EDITED BY HASSAN MAHAMDALLIE

DEFENDING MULTICULTURALISM

A GUIDE FOR THE MOVEMENT
EDITED BY HASSAN MAHAMDALLIE

Defending Multiculturalism: A Guide for the Movement
Edited by Hassan Mahamdallie

First published in September 2011 by Bookmarks Publications
c/o 1 Bloomsbury Street, London WC1B 3QE
© Bookmarks Publications except where otherwise stated

Cover design by Mohammed Ali (Aerosolarabic) www.aerosolarabic.com
Front cover photograph by Jess Hurd © Jess Hurd/reportdigital.co.uk
Back cover image adapted from an original artwork by Zita Holbourne ©
Typeset by Bookmarks Publications
Printed by Halstan Printing Group

ISBN 978 1 90519 284 7

CONTENTS

EDITOR'S ACKNOWLEDGEMENTS

The editor would like to thank all those involved in the initial Defend Multiculturalism, Don't Let Cameron Divide Us petition and campaign, including all the signatories. Thank you to all the authors and artists for their generous contributions that make up this book.

A special thanks to Martin Smith, whose idea this project was. Many thanks also to commissioning editor at Bookmarks Sally Campbell and to Peter Robinson for typesetting and page design. A big thank you to Mohammed Ali (Aerosolarabic) for the cover design.

We all sincerely hope that *Defending Multiculturalism* will be a guide for the movement.

Preface

PETER HAIN

This publication comes at a critical time. When the British prime minister attacks our multicultural society in (of all places) Munich, that's a concern.

When he does so on the same day as the English Defence League is swaggering aggressively through Luton preaching fascism and racism and he doesn't condemn them, that's downright frightening.

When in addition he says that "muscular liberalism" should replace multi-racialism and multiculturalism, has he the slightest idea that his words are an open invitation to the EDL and the BNP to say we have a friend in high places? Indeed they did precisely that.

A lot of our politicians in the Westminster Club do not have the faintest idea that that speech by David Cameron, coinciding as it did with the EDL demonstration, caused fear to ripple through every Muslim household in Britain.

Politicians should not play fast and loose with issues of race and religion in a way that scapegoats minorities.

Genuine multiculturalism celebrates, not simply the importance of difference, but also common British identity, common citizenship. And it cherishes dialogue and tolerance between different communities, races and faiths.

Britain, whether the right wing likes it or not, is a genuinely multicultural society. That's our history, especially post-Second World War, of people of different races and faiths being encouraged to settle here.

That's why we won the bid for the 2012 Olympics. The International Olympic Committee saw before it in the British delegation a microcosm of the world: multi-race, multi-faith, multi-identity, all lobbying for the same British cause.

In truth we are stronger standing together in our multicultural society, and we are weaker divided.

Defending our multicultural way of life is important, because it enriches us all, from football to poetry, from music to IT. It's impossible to conceive of a BNP or EDL all-white Britain. It would be unrecognisable from the Britain we know and experience today.

That's why defending Muslims and opposing Islamophobia is vital. Why confronting the poison of the BNP and the EDL is essential. Why demonstrating and arguing and organising through Unite Against Fascism is crucial.

The multiculturalism we enjoy today was defended and advanced through struggles against racism and uniting communities, from demonstrations against the Blackshirts attacking Jews in the 1930s, to the mass movement mobilised by the Anti Nazi League in the 1970s and 1980s.

From a childhood during the anti-apartheid struggle in South Africa, to helping lead the Anti-Apartheid Movement in Britain, to fighting against racism and the far right, I have always put this struggle at the centre of my political life.

Today we face a serious threat from the EDL and the BNP. The far right is on the rise and the march right across Europe, feeding off mounting popular grievances caused by the banking crisis, the economic recession and savage cuts in public services and jobs.

In Britain the way the Tory Lib Dem Government is slashing public spending is making our poorest communities even poorer, in turn providing easy targets for those who cannot get jobs or houses to scapegoat people of a different race or faith. This divide-and-rule politics has always been a trademark of the right.

We must resist it by standing up proudly for our multicultural society.

◆ Labour MP Peter Hain is the author of the biography *Mandela* (Spruce, 2010).

AVAES MOHAMMAD: CLASH

The haves the have nots
The haves but will not
The woulds but could not
The coulds but would not

The haves but think not
The thinks but ask not
The asks but know not
The knows but care not

The tongue that speaks lots
But voice that's heard not
The tongue that's heard lots
But speech that tells not

Apparent stand-offs
Between us and rest of
The world that thinks not
In terms that suit us

The lies we spread lots
Of foreign despots
That wish to kill us
So must be killed off

The heads that bow not
The hands that shake not
When holding sling-shots
When facing gun-shots

The view that's changed not
From colonial plots
Civilising dark flocks
To get what they've got

The books that teach not
Each phrase a new knot
Claim cultures move not
And stand as fixed blocks

The books that flow past
Borders and don't stop
Make ours who once were
People we knew not

A choice we've all got
Be held or hold off
Embrace what's known not
Knowing we know not

Or claim we share not
And so we grow not
What's different trust not
And let it be not

The haves the have nots
The haves but will not
The ones that call shots
The ones that get shot

That is the only clash of civilisations I know

REACHING FOR RACISM
THAT SPEECH IN MUNICH

Defending multiculturalism: An introduction

HASSAN MAHAMDALLIE

David Cameron and his coalition government have declared war on the multicultural way of life that all of us, black and white, of faith and no faith, have struggled so hard to build, nurture and strengthen.

This collection of essays, poems, photographs and artwork is a direct response to that attack, as well as a resource by which to defend the multiculturalism we enjoy and indeed to extend it. It is a measure of the severity of the attack that all of the contributors to *Defending Multiculturalism* have given their labour freely and with enthusiasm.

Defending Multiculturalism arose out of the shock that rippled through the Muslim community and the anti-racist, anti-fascist and trade union movements at the speech David Cameron made early in 2011. In the days following Cameron's "End of Multiculturalism" speech a group of signatories, including those who have contributed to this book, put their names to a letter published in the *Guardian* newspaper. It read:

> We believe David Cameron's statement that multiculturalism has failed was a dangerous declaration of intent (Blaming the victims, Editorial, 7 February). His speech was reminiscent of Margaret Thatcher's infamous 1978 statement that Britain was "being swamped by alien cultures". He has branded Britain's Muslims as the new "enemy within" in the same way as Thatcher attacked the miners and trade unions.
>
> David Cameron is attempting to drive a wedge between different communities by linking Britain's multicultural society with terrorism and national security. His speech was made on the same day as the

English Defence League brought its bigotry and violence to the streets of Luton. Mr Cameron's aim is simple as it is crude—to deflect the anger against his government's cuts from the bankers and on to the Muslim community. The prime minister is aping attacks by other European leaders like France's Nicolas Sarkozy, who passed legislation banning the veil, and Angela Merkel, who has also made statements denouncing multiculturalism in Germany. We believe our multicultural society and the respect and solidarity it is built on is a cause for pride, and we reject any moves by this government to undermine and destroy it.

We must not allow this coalition government to turn the tide back to the days when it was acceptable, through ignorance and fear, for people with a different religion, culture or skin colour to be scapegoated and treated as inferior or outsiders.

The letter drew such support that it was made into a national petition going on to quickly attract over 7,000 signatures. Enough money was pledged to have the statement republished as a half-page advert in the *Guardian*. Shortly afterwards, a successful rally was held in central London, with the audience hearing a broad alliance of speakers including Edie Friedman, founder of the Jewish Council for Racial Equality, George Galloway, Billy Hayes from the CWU post workers' union, Kevin Courtney from the teachers' NUT, Dilowar Khan from the East London Mosque, Martin Smith from Love Music Hate Racism, former children's laureate Mike Rosen, poet Avaes Mohammed, Kanjay Sesay from the National Union of Students, Zita Holbourne from the TUC Race Relations Committee and Sabby Dhalu from Unite Against Fascism and One Society Many Cultures.

The London rally was followed by similar meetings around the country addressed by figures such as Salma Yaqoob from the Respect party, Professor Danny Dorling (author of the important book *Injustice: Why Social Inequality Persists*), and speakers from the Green Party, Gypsy and Traveller groups, Muslim organisations, anti-racists and the trade union movement.

In the autumn of 2011 a series of Defend Multiculturalism meetings will be set up around the country, using discussion around the essays in this book as way of taking the campaign further.

Why has Cameron's speech rung such clear alarm bells?

It could be argued that Cameron is only travelling further down the repressive road mapped out by Tony Blair as part of his bloody "war on terror". The deafening silence from New Labour, apart from opposition frontbenchers distancing themselves from Labour MP Sadiq Khan's condemnation of Cameron, was indeed wretched. The nature of subsequent debates led by the right in the Labour Party give little hope for the near future.

We all know that the Tories like nothing more than a spoonful or two of bigotry with their politics, but Cameron's speech marked a step-change in state racism.

It was on 5 February 2011 that Cameron delivered his carefully crafted speech at a security conference in Munich with the intention of declaring the end of multiculturalism (as if it was in his power to do so). The speech's intent was to drive a wedge through our society precisely at the same time as working people face the greatest attack on their living standards for generations.

The reactionary nature of Cameron's Munich speech was revealed by those who applauded it and the reasons they gave for their backing. Germany's Angela Merkel, Spain's Jose Maria Aznar and France's Nicholas Sarkozy all rushed to endorse his pronouncements. All agreed that multiculturalism has had its day (not that any of those states had ever actually implemented multicultural policies) and that their Muslim populations had better behave themselves.

The speech also made Cameron new admirers from the cesspool that is Europe's far right. Marine Le Pen, who leads France's fascist Front National, was overjoyed: "It is exactly this type of statement that has barred us from public life [in France] for 30 years... I sense an evolution at European level, even in classic governments. I can only congratulate him."

The band of Nazis, soccer hooligans, racists and thugs that make up the English Defence League, busy terrorising Luton's Muslims *on the very same day* that Cameron chose to make his speech, couldn't believe their good fortune. Their website commented: "Cameron has now taken that first step towards seriously addressing the threat that certain forms of Islam pose to this country. So, thank you Dave. The speech is a landmark event. It marks an important departure from the last 30 years of government thinking."

The speech and its reception were signals that the hard right and attendant Islamophobes inside and around the Tory party, sensing that the austerity-driven government needed a scapegoat, had won out. In the face of this, Tory chair Baroness Warsi's speech made a month before arguing that Islamophobia was the last "respectable" racism, applauded by British Muslim organisations, fades into irrelevance.

The implications of Cameron's speech began to be played out four months later when the coalition government produced its revamped "Preventing Terrorism" strategy, breathing new life into a divisive and destructive programme of work conjured up by New Labour as a diversion from the consequences of Blair's wars on the people of Afghanistan and Iraq.

The new Prevent programme not only recast Britain's Muslims, their religion and their organisations as "suspect", it went further than its previous incarnation. Its ramifications are severe. Any Muslim or Muslim organisation that is deemed by the state and its authorities as having "extreme" views will be regarded as treasonous and supporting terrorism—regardless of whether they do or not. The government is cementing into policy the utterly false notion that the vast majority of Muslim organisations—which are of course non-violent—are now to be viewed as merely a staging post to suicide bombing.

The only Muslim groups free from scrutiny will be those fostered by the state as client organisations—a handful of which were set up by the New Labour government as pretend spokespeople for "moderate Islam". For the powers-that-be Muslims will be herded into two pens: "Good Muslims" and "Bad Muslims", with this binary played out through criminal and social policy and funding streams. (To save them the trouble they can put me in the latter category.)

The effect of this "loyalty test" will be to place all Muslims under suspicion, forcing them at every turn to declare their allegiance to a meaningless set of "British values". The cornerstone of our liberties—innocent until proven guilty—will be set on its head for the men, women and children of two million of our fellow citizens. No one else but Muslims (for the time being) will be put to this test. We are entering an era of Orwellian thought-crime—to think or believe something is treated exactly the same as acting it out.

What follows is an exchange between a Radio 4 presenter and Lib Dem peer Lord Carlile, the self-important government Prevent advisor and eager shredder of our civil liberties:

> *Presenter*: To be clear, in future the government will take the view that if you call for British soldiers overseas to be killed—if you say you think that's a good idea—that's as serious in the view of the government as actually going to Afghanistan and carrying it out?
> *Carlile*: And your problem with that is?

You don't have to agree with terrorism to feel the chill as Carlile flippantly endorses a historic attack on freedom of speech. We are all being shoved rapidly down a very slippery slope towards the destruction of our human rights.

The Prevent document itself gives the game away. At the start it states "We remain absolutely committed to protecting freedom of speech in this country. But preventing terrorism will mean challenging extremist (and non-violent) ideas that are part of a terrorist ideology". Then later on it admits that this is in contravention of human rights: "The holding of extremist views is protected by Article 10 of [the] European Convention of Human Rights and cannot be addressed through criminal law". In other words, the government wants to pass legislation to restrict our freedom of speech, and is only stopped from doing so by international laws passed to protect ordinary people's voices against dictatorial regimes.

It was extraordinary therefore to hear Home Secretary Teresa May announcing the new Prevent programme, an update of the Thatcher era witch-hunter Norman Tebbit's "cricket test":

> If organisations do not support the values of democracy, human rights, equality before the law, participation in society—if they do not accept these fundamental and universal values—then we will not work with them and we will not fund them.

Go through the list: democracy, human rights, equality before the law, participation in society (is it now a crime not to "participate"?). It doesn't take much effort to compare the actions and beliefs of this government with all of these "fundamental and universal values" and find it utterly wanting.

The Prevent document makes fantastical reading. Nowhere does it admit the truth that is as plain as the nose on Cameron's face—that the direct cause of terrorist attacks such as 9/11 and 7/7 is the foreign policy of Western governments, principally the US and Britain, in the Middle East. The perpetual war against the population of Afghanistan, the criminal and barbaric assault against Iraq, the bombing of Libya, along with the continued propping-up of Arab dictators friendly to Western interests, has produced its asymmetrical reaction.

Instead the government has reached for the old tool of the powerful—draw attention away from what you are doing by blaming those you are oppressing. According to Prevent and government thinking, terrorism arises out of an ill-defined "extremist ideology", and any Muslims who think otherwise and say it are merely revelling in their own imagined "victimhood". It is precisely because of this lie at the very heart of Prevent that we face the prospect of the attacks on Muslims by the government and the racist organisations who ride the tide of hostility, to continue and gather pace. That is why all those opposed to this scapegoating must argue and organise against it now.

However, Prevent is only one manifestation of a wider project. This coalition government is using anti-Muslim racism as part of its project to weaken the ties of unity and solidarity that exist between those under attack from its austerity measures. For the Tories the attack on multiculturalism is in essence a class-driven offensive.

Cameron's message in Munich was bulked out by the usual lies that surround his worldview. Cameron cited the example of "Islamic fundamentalists" taking over British prisons. There is no evidence whatsoever that this has happened in any British prison. It's a complete invention. Cameron also resurrected the myth that Muslim communities have failed to confront forced marriages—despite the fact that you would be hard-pressed to find an individual Muslim advocating this.

His attack on "failed multiculturalism" also rested on a bed of falsehoods. The notion that multiculturalism was ever an official state policy is simply not true. Where local councils have funded a few facilities for minority ethnic groups, the overall thrust has been to give them "a leg-up" and the confidence to engage with society on the basis of equality.

Study after study shows that Britain's Muslims are integrated, as much as they are allowed, into wider society. Muslims are anti-war—with all the fundamentally decent values that implies—alongside the great majority of British people.

Given that most Muslims are working class, they are patently more integrated into society than the British upper classes, who take pride in their separation from "the unwashed masses". How many of us can say that we have a community-minded millionaire city banker living next door?

Demographic studies have shown that it is overwhelmingly the fear of racist hostility that has acted to discourage black and Asian people moving into majority white areas. The coalition's attack on the poor and the stamping on working class aspirations to a university education will do more to isolate communities than any other force in contemporary British life. Cameron claimed that multiculturalism had left young Muslims "feeling rootless". The truth is that if some young Muslims feel shut out of society, it is the result of poverty, unemployment and racism compounded by hostility to Islam.

When communities have been divided, the root cause has rarely been people's religious beliefs. It was racist local council policies that led to segregated housing, for example. In the north of England it was employers, notoriously the mill owners, who deliberately segregated their workforce along ethnic lines as a profitable ploy to divide and rule. And it has been the established political parties who have traditionally sought to treat minority ethnic voters as homogenous electoral blocs, and "community leaders" as the agency to deliver their backing, even if it meant playing one group off against another.

We should never forget the words of the campaigning journalist Paul Foot, writing in 1965 about the threat racist demagogue and Tory MP Enoch Powell then represented:

Hassan Mahamdallie

Politics can drive the knife home or remove its menace... No one can underestimate the danger of that choice. The tiger of racialism, once unleashed, knows no master. It devours its liberators and its prey with equal ferocity.

The contributions that make up *Defending Multiculturalism* are divided into three sections. The first section is made up of political, academic, creative and personal responses to Cameron's speech. Ken Livingstone makes a persuasive argument that London's success and recognition as a world city rests on a bedrock of dynamic multiculturalism. Along the way he articulates a warning against those in the Labour Party who want to take the whole debate on immigration and diversity in a rightwards direction. Liz Fekete from the Institute of Race Relations and author of the highly regarded book, *A Suitable Enemy* offers the reader an eye-opening and forensic examination of the way in which European states are lining up behind Islamophobic and xenophobic policies that are in turn fuelling the growth of far right and anti-Muslim parties across the continent. Zita Holbourne's defiant and celebratory contribution moves from a personal, and highly political, defence of multiculturalism to a very practical guide for trade union activists who wish to take the defence of our way of life into our workplaces and union organisations. Michael Rosen is one of our finest poets and is a tireless activist for equality. His contribution consists of a lively examination of the truths that underline "culture", complemented by two of his most popular poems.

Professor Tariq Modood is an internationally renowned academic and founding Director of the Centre for the Study of Ethnicity and Citizenship at the University of Bristol. He has led from the front in the call for a rational and informed debate around multiculturalism, and has proved to be an effective debunker of the myths pumped out by hostile politicians and media commentators. Tariq has contributed a new analysis of multiculturalism and its opponents, and one that attempts to clear away the smoke to enable us to see the issues more clearly. Sabby Dhalu, joint secretary of Unite Against Fascism, actively involved at a national level in combating the threat posed by the BNP and the EDL, outlines the threat posed by the attack on Muslims across

Europe and lays out the need for the new campaigning organisation One Society Many Cultures. The concluding essay in the first section is by Professor Danny Dorling, who has done so much to show that inequality is a political and economic choice and not a natural and inevitable state of affairs and to explode the myths behind the idea that Muslims are somehow naturally self-segregating. For this book he has updated an important study he originally wrote for the Runnymede Trust. In it he definitively takes on the wrong argument that the "white working class" are somehow the casualties of multiculturalism.

The middle section of the book reaches back into history and draws out some of the political lessons that we need to defend multiculturalism. Dr Edie Friedman, founder of the Jewish Council for Racial Equality, demonstrates that this is not the first time that the British establishment has reached for racism against "the other". Edie describes how Jewish refugees fleeing persecution over a century ago met with overwhelming antisemitism in Britain, hostility that was to have terrible consequences. Gary McFarlane's wide-ranging historical study takes apart the notion that humanity is divided by separate distinct cultures based on national boundaries, and by using the National Anthem challenges the falsehood that we are "all in it together". Benjamin Zephaniah contributes a poetic take on Gary's analysis with his celebrated poem, "The British". Hassan Mahamdallie tells the hidden history of the working class struggles of Britain's Muslims, and Colin Wilson concludes the section with an authoritative contemporary and historical examination of the relationship between this country's imperial past and racism and homophobia.

The final section combines trenchant analysis of the dangers facing us with strategies for how we can take the struggle to defend multiculturalism forwards. Respect leader and Birmingham councillor Salma Yaqoob discusses the impact of Cameron's attacks on our Muslim communities, the reality of life in the mixed communities that make up our cities, and ends with a vision built on unity and common purpose. Martin Smith, who is in the forefront of the fight against the BNP and the EDL, gives an in-depth analysis of the nature of the English Defence League, its direct links to the BNP and the very serious danger it currently represents. Martin's article adds up to a warning we ignore at our peril. Yuri Prasad's interview with Dilowar Khan, the director of the east London Mosque and the London Muslim Centre, is both a fascinating account of growing up facing racism in East London and an inspiring example of how unity forged on the ground between Muslim and non-Muslim can oppose and defeat the threat of the far right. The post workers' union general secretary and anti-fascist campaigner Billy Hayes contributes an important article on the central role our trade unions have to play in the struggle. He takes to task both the Tories and the right wing of the Labour Party and concludes that the trade unions must not give an inch to bigotry. Weyman Bennett, joint secretary of Unite Against Fascism, concludes with an account of the struggle to establish our multicultural society and the need for a strategy that can mobilise people on two fronts: firstly against the threat of the far right, and secondly against the softer and more sophisticated racist ideas espoused by Cameron and those commentators who support him. What we need, Weyman argues, is a combined and overlapping "militant anti-fascist activity on the ground with a principled anti-racist defence of the multicultural society".

Along the way the reader will appreciate the role that creativity has to play in the struggle. There are two pointed and amusing cartoons by Tim and poetry from spoken word artist and playwright Avaes Mohammad and from Zita Holbourne. *Defending Multiculturalism* highlights the visual studies of east London chronicler Rehan Jamil and the vital work of photographer and campaigner Kelvin Williams.

A final point. Some writers have characterised British society over the decades as "drifting" towards multiculturalism, a kind of benign evolution towards integration. However, this view obscures the ways in which we got where we are today.

The progress towards a multicultural society has always advanced through anti-racist struggles large and small, everyday and historic; from the defence of black and Asian immigrants against race riots, the battles of black youth against the "sus" laws and racist policing of the Notting Hill Carnival, the fight to turn the trade unions into bastions of anti-racism, the struggle of school teachers and students to enjoy anti-racist teaching, the multi-racial riots that erupted in our inner-cities under Thatcher, down to the growth of a multicultural youth culture and stubborn defence of our communities from attack by Moseley's fascists, the National Front, the British Movement, the BNP and the EDL.

The fight of the Asian workers at the Grunwicks factory in the late 1970s led by the recently deceased Jayaben Desai would have been lesser but for the physical support of the Yorkshire miners on the west London picket line, and the 1984-85 fight of the miners would have been lesser but for the solidarity delivered by miners' support groups including the black and LGBT communities of London.

If you blow away the smokescreen, at the root of Cameron's attack is a profound hostility to our multicultural society and a desire to undermine the unity that is its strength. His "muscular liberalism" represents an urge to drive a wedge between us, at the very point when we need to stand together against the coalition's attacks. It is precisely the values that have built our multicultural society that we will need to use for its defence.

◆ If you would like to order more copies of this book, or to organise a Defend Multiculturalism meeting in your area, place of worship or workplace please contact Unite Against Fascism:

Unite Against Fascism
PO Box 36871
London WC1X 9XT
020 7801 2782
Info@uaf.org.uk

In praise of multicultural London

KEN LiVINGSTONE

London is the most international and diverse city in the world. This is a description of both the diversity of its population and the functioning of its economy. Moreover each is a function of the other. You cannot have London's global economic role without necessarily and inevitably having a global population, and this international population feeds its global economic success.

This international and diverse character of the city is a product of both its historic and contemporary position.

London developed as a global hub initially as a great northern European port, competing with the port cities of the Netherlands to be the premier trading and banking depot for the sea routes from the Mediterranean and beyond. From its earliest history it was a diverse and open city, welcoming merchants and seafarers, Huguenots and Jews, South American revolutionaries and iconoclastic scientists and thinkers, and refugees from across the globe.

With the rise of the British Empire it became a centre of political, economic and cultural exchange with the Far East, India and Africa, bringing further great waves of migration to the city, and laying the basis for its contemporary role in a globalised world economy.

Now it is a centre of global finance and business services, the most international major financial centre in the world, and a centre of the global creative industries and research in life sciences and pharmaceuticals. Situated halfway between the time-zones of Asia and the eastern US and a gateway to Europe, London's success is based on the international and outward-looking character of the city.

The immense diversity of its population has both contributed to its success in this role and is an inevitable consequence of it.

That is why I am so unrelentingly hostile to all those who argue that our problems are rooted in immigration or that multiculturalism has failed. Not only do these attitudes fly in the face of the reality of London, but if implemented they would destroy the basis of its future prosperity and success, and therefore the well-being and living standards of all Londoners. Moreover, given the disproportionate contribution of London and the south east to the whole country's GDP and tax basis, it actually strikes at the well-being and prosperity of all our citizens.

In its extremely international character, while London is in advance of other cities in the world—internationally the most similar city is New York, which is also highly diverse (though not as diverse as London)—and the most successful city in the world by many measures, it is merely at the leading edge of what is happening to major cities the world over.

Every great city worldwide is facing the growing international diversity of their populations, they are just less far along the road than London or New York. From Mumbai to Shanghai, Singapore to Moscow, Sao Paolo to Johannesburg, global companies are bringing global workforces, and people are migrating temporarily or permanently, regionally and internationally, to seek work, set up businesses, take advantage of growth and success, seek a better life or simply one that is different from that they grew up in. This is a vital process economically and creatively: to be successful cities, companies and populations have to be in touch with the most up to date ideas and developments taking place across the globe. That is why the world's most successful companies—like GlaxoSmithKline, Google or Apple, for example—look globally for their scientists, researchers, product developers, designers and managers. To demand they confine their skill search to one group of narrowly nationally defined workers is to put a brake on innovation, the interchange of ideas and fruitful dialogue and would just lead to underachievement. Because of this, global companies will simply choose not to base themselves in cities and countries where they face such restrictions, with all the consequent loss of local jobs. And such companies will be unlikely to develop in the first place in a context of such restrictions.

It is because Britain—partly as a result of its most definitely far from glorious role in establishing a global empire—had a relatively open immigration policy for most of the 20th century that London has been able to move from being a great imperial port to a world centre of global trade, finance and commerce and remain a globally successful and dynamic city, despite Britain's overall relative decline.

In an age of globalisation—predicated on the free movement of finance and trade—it is inevitable that the trend will be towards the international free movement of labour. If governments and reactionary elements try to resist this, by putting up legal barriers and guarding their borders, they will always only partly succeed. But they can turn their societies in on themselves, churn up conflict and face their populations away from the rest of the world and all that is most dynamic and fruitful. And this together with the degree of their actual success will undermine economic growth. That is why the US—until recently the world's most successful economy—has always been defined as a country of immigrants, with a rather open immigration policy most of the time.

Even without this economic imperative, it is quite impossible to believe that in an age of globalised production, trade, financial transactions and transferable skills, coupled with the modern age's ease of international travel, that human beings—who are by nature curious and exploratory—will not increasingly live in different and multiple countries in the course of their lives.

In other words, all those—politicians, pundits and opinion-formers—who seek to appeal to those who have found most difficulty in adjusting to our constantly changing world and society by saying that we can turn in on ourselves, shut out the "foreign", and be uniformly "British" not only play to the most backward fears and prejudices. They are also encouraging their audiences to pursue a policy that would undermine their own future prosperity and standard of living.

Britain is irreversibly a highly diverse society. The clock cannot be turned back on this. It has been increasingly so for several hundred years. If we try to define British culture—favourite dish chicken tikka masala, most well-known musicians the Beatles and the Rolling

Stones who popularised music rooted in Black American blues, most iconic food the Jewish-originating fish and chips, drinking Irish stout and European lager—it either becomes a catalogue of the influence of that diversity, or has to appeal to a non-existent shared culture of Morris dancers, warm beer, cricket and Greensleeves, which is fine for pageantry but is not the culture that forms most people's lives. Or it becomes the English Defence League type nationalism of the football hooligan that defines our culture as male-dominated, aggressive, bullying, drunken and foul-mouthed.

The reality of contemporary British culture is that it is already deeply formed by international influences, brought to us both by waves of migrants who are now long-term settled communities and by the functioning of the international market that brings us music, film, TV series and many other elements of popular culture from all over the world.

Moreover, our society—as with those across the world—is going to become more diverse, not less, as the future unfolds.

Multiculturalism is therefore in the first place not a policy response but a simple description of the character of our society and the understanding we all need to have of how it is going to develop in the future, due to the nature of the world we live in. The issue is how we live with the consequences of that, what are the challenges and what are the advantages, and how do we deal with them.

Our role as politicians should be to help our populations face that future with confidence, not encourage them to turn in on themselves and believe a pretence that at some point everyone can be forced to integrate into a universal shared "Britishness" which doesn't exist.

Britain, of course, does have an extraordinary depth of culture—from Shakespeare to Pinter, Jane Austen and Dickens, Milton and Burns, Turner to the pre-Raphaelites, this country has produced a range of art that is on a par with that produced by any other nation and is internationally appreciated and loved. We also have an enviable heritage, from Stonehenge to the Tower of London, Hampton Court to Rievaulx Abbey, St Paul's to St Pancras station.

These historic strengths were born of the fusion of the international ideas and influences of the time. Who could imagine Shakespeare writing his plays without the influence of the Italian renaissance, the European explorations of America and all the new ideas breaking into the world in the 17th century? In the same way as then, our heritage and historical culture—themselves rooted in past diversity and "multiculturalism"—are a springboard to the future, a platform to reach out to the world, a basis for new meetings and fusions between cultures in our society.

While Britain has a great historical culture, it is also constantly reinventing itself and creating things that are new—the Gherkin and the London Eye are now as internationally recognised parts of the London skyline as Tower Bridge. Quirky British films—such as *Bend it Like Beckham* or *Four Weddings and a Funeral*—still storm the world's cinemas. Our popular music constantly breaks new ground.

This combination is at the core of London and Britain's cultural strength. But this is a product of the open, diverse and international character of the most dynamic and leading parts of the country—inevitably its cities, and foremost among them London. It is the interaction of the extraordinary depth of London's—or any great city's—accumulated cultural assets with its contemporary character looking outward and forward to the world and the future that creates their dynamism.

If we take the case of London, we can see that this character of the city—based on the immense diversity of its population—has to be defended, nurtured and celebrated, so that all our citizens, whatever their background, feel invigorated, affirmed and wanted culturally and economically.

That means explaining—and helping our whole population understand and celebrate—that our culture is forged from the combination of the historic past and the specific contributions that have been and are continually being brought to it by different parts of its population—young and old, Christian, Jew, Hindu, Muslim, Asian, African, male and female, straight and gay. These and many other communities, ethnicities, faiths and sensitivities have created a British culture which is defined by the diversity of its citizens, who can live at ease with each other and flourish in an environment of constant change.

Of course, this is easier said than achieved. But the first step has to be to understand that this character of our culture is irreversible, is positive, is a source of strength and our society is more integrated if we celebrate this rather than futilely oppose it or mourn some past, entirely imaginary, golden age when we all thought the same and liked the same things.

That is why, for example, I initiated the free public festivals on Trafalgar Square for St Patrick's Day, Diwali, the Russian Winter Festival, Eid, St George's Day and so on. It was a message to the communities concerned that they and their culture were welcomed and they should feel at home. And it was a message to all Londoners that these different cultural experiences are for us all to share, adding to the richness of all of our lives. This approach contributed to the reasons why, in our polling of Londoners every year from 2000 onwards, we never got less than 86 percent of respondents saying they considered the diversity of London was either a positive or very positive feature of the city.

I firmly believe that the core liberal principle—that we should all have the freedom to live, believe and express our culture as we please as long as it does not prevent anyone else doing likewise—is not only a necessary basis for an integrated society, but it is what everyone fundamentally wants.

People have migrated to towns and cities because they are more culturally dynamic and diverse, offer greater choices, and allow people to live the lives that they choose. While for those that choose it, a country village and a small, close community is ideal, others want variety, multiple cultural possibilities, different job opportunities, varied friends, lifestyles and relationships. Diversity is not just created by the arrival of international migrants, different religions and global cultures; it is fundamental to our modern way of life. As society has become more affluent, more choices have become available and people want the opportunity to experience them. And the experiences people choose are increasingly drawn from range of global options, because multimedia communications, the internet, digital sources and e-commerce mean we aren't just reliant on the BBC Home Service and the magazines stocked in our local newsagent for our cultural choices.

This is an exciting time to be alive. Exponential times, when the whole world and all its cultures are within our reach, wherever we live. Times where each new technological advance gives us more options, more choices, more knowledge, more experiences. And inevitably this means our culture globalises and becomes more mixed, not just because people come here, but because we reach out to all that the world has to offer.

So why, given this is intrinsic to the world we live in, is there the deep assault on multiculturalism, led by the Tories, echoed by the BNP and EDL, but also advocated by some in the Labour Party?

Why did David Cameron make that speech in Munich on 5 February 2011 arguing that multiculturalism had failed? And that British Muslims who were refusing to conform to "British values" had to be confronted with what he described as a "muscular liberalism", but which actually amounted to a definition of illiberalism? He defined "Islamic extremism" with a broad catch-all and not only threatened the funding, but said the government would not even talk to any Muslim group that did not measure up to his definition of "British values".

I don't believe David Cameron made this speech because he was carried away with the myths and prejudices that do afflict sections of the population. He knows that immigration into Britain is not uniquely high and is largely balanced by net migration out of the country. He is aware of the hard evidence of the positive impact of migration on our economy. Government research has found that a 1 percent increase in the ratio of immigrants leads to an increase of up to 0.4 percent in average earnings. In 2006 government estimates showed that immigration added a net £6 billion to GDP growth—creating new jobs, not reducing them.

Nor was he unaware of the polling evidence that shows British Muslims, for example, are more patriotic, more law-abiding and feel more civic responsibility than white British people.

He was not responding to a genuine set of political concerns. He was using a time-honoured tactic of right wing politicians whose policies are undermining people's standard of living, destroying jobs and creating insecurity.

The trick is to attempt to protect your electoral position by shifting the anger onto innocent scapegoats—immigrants, asylum seekers, Muslims, Gypsies, black people. It was no coincidence that the speech came at the point that polls put the Tories behind Labour for the first time since the general election.

It is exactly the same tactic as has been attempted by Sarkozy in France, who has responded to his plummeting position in the polls with forced deportations of Roma and a ban on the less than 2,000 women in France who wear the full face veil.

So far all that Sarkozy has achieved is to boost the support for Marine Le Pen's neo-fascist Front National, which is precisely why this is such a dangerous game.

Sadly, this politics of the gutter is what we have come to expect from the Tories when they face electoral decline. The struggling last Tory government before the 1997 election took exactly this course, introducing draconian anti-immigration and anti-asylum legislation, unleashing a wave of harassment of Britain's black communities and encouraging a daily scare campaign focused on asylum seekers in the Tory press.

As the impact of austerity bites, these trends are likely to deepen. As sections of the population find their living standards devastated and unemployment looming, and in the absence of clear alternatives, some can be persuaded that this is the fault not of bankers and Tory politicians, but must be due to immigrants or some other section of the population. Such views are reinforced by the constant media scare campaigns against Muslims and Islam—sharia law, halal meat, the burqa debate and many others—or against immigrants of any variety. And as the Tories plunge in the polls there will be more speeches like that in Munich, which put society's ills down to multiculturalism, diversity, immigrants and Muslims.

Whether this works or not in bolstering support for the Tory party, what it will certainly do is legitimise attacks on minority communities—especially today's demons, Britain's Muslim communities.

In this context it is particularly worrying that at this political moment a current has emerged within Labour that appears to argue for concessions to this type of agenda. Maurice Glasman and the small but influential current around him describe their approach as "Blue Labour", arguing, among other things, that Labour has to admit it "lied" on immigration and that it is wrong to argue that "everyone who comes is equal and has an equal status with people who are here".[1]

Parts of this current have even suggested Labour must engage with the supporters of the neo-Nazi EDL and their concerns.

Much of the argument of this group—and others including, surprisingly, the anti-fascist group Searchlight in much of their recent material[2]—is based on the idea that there is a crisis of either English or British identity in what they describe as the "white working class". This "identity crisis", it is alleged, is why swathes of working class people stopped voting Labour since 1997 (Labour lost 5 million primarily working class votes between 1997 and 2010) and why sections of such people are attracted to the simplistic, racist views of forces like the EDL. They go on to suggest Labour has to adjust to this identity crisis by more strongly asserting a specifically "English" or British labour movement identity, and be more prepared to concede that "immigration" is a fundamental problem.

This argument not only opens the door to racism, but it is also profoundly wrong. Labour lost 5 million votes in 13 years because it squandered the goodwill of the electorate by the Iraq and Afghanistan wars and by a series of economic policies that hit working class living standards. Finally it was Brown's disastrous abolition of the 10p tax band that destroyed the recovery of Labour's vote that had followed the departure of Blair. This was no crisis of "Englishness"; it was a crisis of confidence among sections of Labour's core vote about whether Labour really stood for their interests, which the U-turn restoring the reduced tax rate to a majority of those affected was not enough to overcome. Despite the claims of the Tories, it was not the banking crisis either. Voters perfectly understood that it was the bankers who had created the banking crisis, and the intervention of the state prevented a worse crisis. Even the national debt—the so-called "overspent national credit card"—was not a central issue for voters. Voters are primarily motivated by the fundamentals of jobs, living standards, welfare provision and other bread and butter issues. There are no votes for Labour in the defence of Englishness or moving to the right on immigration.

Moreover research into the 2010 election results underlines this. Research by Greenberg into the 2010 election proves that Labour did not lose the election because it was "too soft" on immigration.[3] Its research revealed that the 8 percent of voters who had seriously considered voting Labour, but then didn't, were the section of voters who were the least hostile to immigration, the most against cuts and the most in favour of tax increases.

The same research showed that the Lib Dems outpolled Labour only on one issue—their policy of an amnesty for long-term resident illegal immigrants. Tory voters on the other hand were the most hostile to immigration.

Labour lost support because of its failure to deliver improvements in living standards and in reaction to the wars in Iraq and Afghanistan, not because of an "English identity crisis" or failures on immigration. The idea that Labour can recover from these issues by attacking multiculturalism and the interests of Muslims, immigrants and other components of its core support is a dangerous fiction.

The Tory-led coalition's cuts are already having an impact on living standards. Inflation was running—in early 2011—at over 4 percent while wages rose at an average 2 percent. In other words, those in work will not just be feeling worse off; they are worse off. In real terms average wages have fallen back to 2005 levels, the first time that wages have lost five years of value since the 1920s. This is making many sections of the population feel under attack and desperate for a way out. This is not because they are suffering a national identity crisis, but because they are suffering a real decline in their living standards. In such circumstances is all too easy to direct people towards a soft target on the basis of racism and an alleged discrimination against the English, or the "white working class", especially when no economic or political alternatives seem to be on offer.

Rather than cede ground to a racist agenda, it becomes all the more vital to reject this pressure.

The case for why immigration has brought so much value to this country has to be robustly made. Much of the concern about immigration stems from the belief that it creates unemployment. In fact, in 2009 for example, those born overseas accounted for just under 4 million of those in employment in Britain, while British citizens working overseas are currently just under 5 million. The free movement of labour works both ways, and to the benefit of British workers.

The policies of multiculturalism and the defence of diversity have to be at the core of how we develop an integrated and forward-looking society. That does not mean—as the critics of multiculturalism claim—forcing people into categories of race or religion that are not of their choosing, or encouraging culturally segregated communities. People often retreat into segregation because they feel their culture, faith or way of life is not wanted or is considered alien. By strongly celebrating the contribution of different cultures and faiths to our society, we encourage minority communities to feel more part of our society, and we help the majority white population view this diversity as a link to the world and the future, not a threat to a non-existent purely British way of life.

And we have to be entirely clear that racism and racist discrimination really do exist, and really do blight the lives of many people who have a different colour skin, a recognisably Muslim or Afro-Caribbean name, or wear a turban or headscarf. This can take the forms of everyday racist comments, the exclusion from consideration for jobs or university places, under-achievement due to the lowered expectation of society on racial grounds or the absence of appropriate role models, and many others. It can mean discriminatory use of police powers in undue levels of stop and search, elevated incidence of mental health problems due to social exclusion, or media scare stories about halal meat, Africans stealing our homes, equating devout Islam with terrorism, or Eastern European migrants forcing people out of jobs. And it can lead to violence—the desecration of mosques, synagogues and temples, and violence against individuals and their homes.

Racism has to be challenged through practical measures to outlaw discrimination and promote equalities, and through a constant, ruthless and unequivocal argument against every tiny appearance of racism whether in the mainstream or from the explicitly racist far-right.

But above all we have to build confidence in our multicultural and diverse society among all sections of the population. We need to encourage them to realise that our diverse populations are a gateway to the world, to new cultural experiences, to greater choice and freedom for all our population and that they can feel confident precisely because the combination of Britain's great depth of historical culture and its internationalised population gives it the most powerful possible springboard into the future—as long as right wing governments don't turn the country in on itself and into inter-community conflict in a desperate attempt to compensate for the unpopularity of their economic policies.

Understanding the European-wide assault on multiculturalism

LiZ FEKETE

In singling out multiculturalism as a threat to national identity, the leaders of Europe's centre-right parties are using the same kind of rhetoric and specious arguments as Enoch Powell did 40 years ago.

The leaders of mainstream political parties across Europe are, one after the other, announcing the death of multiculturalism in their countries. They tell us of the need to focus instead on national identity. The language, terms and metaphors used subtly (and in some cases crudely) convey a sense of national victimhood, of a majority culture under threat from Muslim minorities and new migrants, who demand special privileges and group rights and refuse to learn the language. What this amounts to is the mobilisation by leading members principally, but not entirely, from the centre-right, of a new popular "common sense" racism against Muslims and foreigners. It is a racism that builds on the proliferation of stereotypical generalisations about "Muslim culture" and the Islamic mind-set that have been generated over the last decade. We are witnessing the revival of arguments first used by Enoch Powell, the Conservative shadow defence secretary who was sacked by Edward Heath in 1968 for his "Rivers of Blood" speech that warned of the dangers posed by mass immigration from the New Commonwealth.[1] Only this time it is not one rogue European politician carrying the flag, but the leaders of centre-right parties now replacing race and immigration with culture and religion as the watchwords. And it is taking place at a time of economic crisis and swingeing cuts, when politicians are desperate to deflect public anger and explain away societal breakdown.

Sarrazin establishes framework

In the last six months leading (mostly) centre-right politicians from Austria, Belgium, France, Germany, Denmark, the Netherlands, Norway and Britain have made speeches, heavily trailed in the media, attacking what British prime minister David Cameron described as "the state doctrine of multiculturalism" or what leading Norwegian conservative Torbjørn Røe Isaksen dismissed as "the naive liberal ideology that people can live together in peace and freedom if they just understand each other well enough".[2] One of the factors driving the current discussion was the publication in Germany in August 2010 of *Deutschland schafft sich ab* (Germany Abolishes Itself), a book by Thilo Sarrazin, a Social Democrat (facing expulsion) and former member (he was sacked) of the Executive Board of the Deutsche Bundesbank. *Deutschland schafft sich ab*, now in its 16th edition, is one of the most read books in Germany since *Mein Kampf*, and its publication has made Sarrazin a millionaire many times over. Many German citizens, particularly among the middle classes, are drawn to Sarrazin's message that a once great nation is now at grave risk of descending into imbecility as immigrants (ie Turks) are genetically of lower intelligence and have higher fertility rates. Since his removal from the board of the Bundesbank, there is increasing support for Sarrazin as a victim of political correctness. Since opinion polls and surveys across Europe routinely show immigration to be a key voter issue and that voters would like to see restrictions on freedom of religion for Muslims, the Sarrazin view poses a very real problem for mainstream politicians. How can they distance themselves from such arguments, clearly based on a revival of Social Darwinism, while not criticising or losing out on the votes of his avid followers?

The solution for many German politicians is to publicly criticise Sarrazin's tone while arguing that when it comes to issues of multiculturalism and integration (of Muslims in particular), Sarrazin might just possibly have a valid point. The debate that Sarrazin unleashed had particular resonance in other German-speaking countries such as Switzerland and Austria. Heinz-Christian Strache, the leader of the extreme-right Freedom Party (with 27 percent of the vote, the second largest party in Vienna) identified himself with the "hunted" Sarrazin who deserved to be given political asylum in Austria.[3] Austria's interior minister, Maria Fekter (Austrian People's Party, ÖVP) went further than other senior conservatives when she too identified herself with Sarrazin, saying she felt "confirmed" by the debate he had initiated.[4] Ever since 2009 Fekter had been under attack from NGOs working in the fields of immigration, refugees, human rights and anti-racism who initially refused to endorse the assimilationist bent of her National Action Plan on Integration (NAPI) and accused her of pandering to Islamophobia and stereotyping Muslims with her emphasis on integration into "values" (suggesting Muslims were a threat to democracy and a state based on the rule of law).[5]

By October 2010 evidence emerged that centre-right politicians across Europe were using the Sarrazin thesis for their own political advantage as a means of introducing a strident assimilationist tone into debates on integration. As country after country plunged into economic crisis and austerity measures loomed, politicians began to identify multiculturalism with social regression and all that was tearing Europe apart. In Germany, where there will be elections in seven of the country's 16 states in 2011, chancellor Angela Merkel, who had previously described Sarrazin's book as "not helpful", set the parameters for discussion. She received a standing ovation from the youth wing of the Christian Democratic Union (CDU) when she declared in a speech in Potsdam on 16 October 2010 that the multicultural society had "utterly failed", that the "multikulti" concept—where people would "live side by side" happily—did not work, and that immigrants needed to do more to integrate, including learning German.[6] Sharing the podium with her in Potsdam was Horst Seehofer, the leader of the Christian Social Union (CSU, the CDU's sister party in Bavaria). Seehofer declared that multiculturalism was dead, adding that the right was committed to a "dominant German culture" (*Leitkultur*).[7]

The outgoing Belgian prime minister Yves Leterme (Christian Democrat and Flemish party, CD&V) stated in a radio interview on 2 November, on the eve of a visit by the German chancellor to Brussels, that he believed Merkel to be right in her remarks in so far as "the policies of integration have not always had the beneficial effects that were expected of them".[8] Other Conservative leaders—from French president

Nicolas Sarkozy, Dutch deputy prime minister Maxine Verhagen, to Danish Liberal Party immigration minister Søren Pind and British prime minister David Cameron—strove to introduce variations on Merkel's theme. Verhagen (Christian Democrat Appeal, CDA) repeated Merkel's claim that multiculturalism had failed, stressing that the Dutch no longer felt at home in their own country while immigrants were not entirely happy either, and called on the Dutch to be prouder of their nation.[9] During a television interview, and using a characteristically impatient tone, Sarkozy declared, "We do not want...a society where communities coexist side by side. If you come to France, you accept to melt into a single community, which is the national community, and if you do not want to accept that, you cannot be welcome in France".[10]

Søren Pind, Denmark's controversial newly appointed immigration minister—a former advisory board member of the notorious Free Press Society[11]—spoke out in favour of assimilation, "as a mixture of cultures does not work". "It should be set in stone," Pind argued, "that Denmark only has room for foreigners that adopt and respect Danish values, norms and traditions; if they don't, they shouldn't be here at all".[12] At an international security conference in Munich on 5 February 2011 (the same day that the far-right English Defence League was marching through Luton), British prime minister David Cameron pitched in, declaring that, "under the doctrine of state multiculturalism, we have encouraged different cultures to live separate lives, apart from each other and the mainstream". The "weakening of our collective identity", furthermore, in what could be defined as "a passively tolerant society", needs to be replaced. With possible reference to the 19th century ethos of muscular Christianity—widely seen as a key engine driver of British colonialism—Cameron argued in favour of a "much more active muscular liberalism".[13]

Multiculturalism as proxy

All the European conservative and liberal party leaders and government ministers, in making these statements, presented themselves as courageous iconoclasts. They imply that multiculturalism has become a form of political correctness against which it is difficult to speak out.

Through what Cameron describes as a "hands-off tolerance" states have conceded too much power to minorities. This idea that, through an excess of generosity and decency, countries have put in place benign multicultural policies, is part of a European-wide myth constructed over the last decade. So too is the notion that politicians are now doing something new in attacking multiculturalism. The term may be the new bogey but it is in fact merely a proxy for Powell's idea of aggressive immigrants and their supporters, out to "overawe and dominate the rest".[14]

Enoch Powell was the British Conservative MP who, in the late 1960s, systematically tried to establish the idea that immigrant workers were an alien horde violating the deepest instincts of a culturally homogenous people. But Powell had admirers on the continent, like the far-right Swiss MP James Schwarzenbach. He called in 1970 for a national referendum on *Überfremdung* (excess of foreigners). Ulrich Schlüer, Schwarzenbach's secretary in those days, is now a Swiss People's Party MP who has taken to campaigning against the excesses of Islam. He was co-president of the Swiss anti-minaret movement that successfully campaigned via a referendum to forbid the construction of minarets.

Powell and Schwarzenbach's flame was kept alive in the UK in the 1980s by a coterie of New Right ideologues (influenced by Friedrich Hayek) including Roger Scruton (founder of the Conservative Philosophy Group), philosophy professor Anthony Flew and head teacher Ray Honeyford—with their supporters in the tabloid press. They drew on the Powellite heritage to launch a concerted attack on cultural pluralism/multiculturalism which they said had given rise to a "reverse racism" and a cultural relativism which posed a threat to the unity of the British nation and its (superior) values and traditions. (The Institute of Race Relations was, for example, attacked for the "bias" in the educational books *Roots* and *Patterns of Racism* it had produced for young people—the media suggested they were so inflammatory as to have ignited riots by black youngsters in north London and extreme-right politicians asked the government to ban them from schools and shops—and for the position taken by its director, A Sivanandan, whose anti-racist "mischief" was specifically deplored in the book *Anti-racism: an Assault on Education and Value* edited by Frank Palmer (The Sherwood Press, 1986).

Again there were similar movements on the continent, such as the *Nouvelle Droite* in France, whose theorists Pierre-André Taguiff and Alain de Benoist attacked anti-racism as a form of xenophobia, and the German academics in the Heidelberg Circle which, in 1982, issued a manifesto arguing that citizenship via naturalisation threatened the ethnic purity of the German *Volk*. For many of today's European advocates of New Right thinking Enoch Powell still remains the iconic figure—a hero in the right wing resistance to immigration and multiculturalism. For instance, the Swiss People's Party MP Oskar Freysinger, in his keynote speech at the December 2010 "Against the Islamisation of Europe" conference in Paris (jointly organised by the fascist Bloc Indentitaire and the Left Riposte Laïque) declared Powell his hero while calling for the "Swiss model" of banning minarets to be exported to other European countries.[15]

Could this attack on multiculturalism have been more coordinated than it appears at first glance—particularly since the European People's Party (the largest grouping in the European Parliament, with 256 members) reacted coolly to the Party of European Socialists' call in October 2010 for all European parliament groupings to adopt a five-point code of conduct on isolating the extreme right? Indeed, since the Dutch conservatives and liberals entered in September 2010 into a coalition government, which is reliant on the support of Geert Wilders's Islamophobic Freedom Party, it has become clear that centre-right parties are preparing for future power-sharing with the extreme right, as tacitly acknowledged by Wilfred Martens, the president of the European People's Party. He said that while conservatives would not work with the extreme-right in the European Parliament, the European People's Party would not dictate to national parties, thus leaving the door open for collaboration at a national, regional and local level.[16] It would seem that the centre-right is responding to the greater coordination of the European anti-immigrant, anti-Muslim electoral forces in preparation for the 2014 European Parliament elections by embracing their arguments. This mirrors the way Margaret Thatcher stole the clothes of the National Front in January 1978 in her notorious "swamping" speech. It is no exaggeration, therefore, to say that the centre-right and the extreme-right are simultaneously building on the anti-immigration, anti-cultural pluralism and anti-anti racism legacy of Powell and the New Right. In line with the whole shift in racism following the war on terror (from anti-black to "civilisational" racism) culture and religion have now replaced biology and colour in a discourse where multiculturalism is being used as the whipping boy, to explain away the impact of the economic and social crisis.

Mobilising the majority, establishing victimhood

In fact, this new New Right discourse closely resembles the old them/us, black/white debate. There is again the playing of the "race card", only now it is the "Islam card" or the "anti-Muslim card" which is most often dealt in electoral politics. It is true that few of the political leaders speak in overtly anti-Muslim, or anti-Islamic terms. But some, like Bavarian prime minister Horst Seehofer or French president Nicolas Sarkozy, certainly do. Seehofer was accused of indulging in "arsonist-style right wing populism" when he railed against the difficulties posed in integrating immigrants from "other cultures", namely "cultural circles" like "Turkey and the Arab countries", and called a halt to all such immigration.[17] As fears grow that the deeply unpopular Nicolas Sarkozy could even be knocked out in the first round of the 2012 presidential elections by the Front National's (FN) Marine Le Pen, and some Union for a Popular Movement (UMP) politicians openly discuss local and regional survival through a UMP-FN pact, Sarkozy announced in March 2011 a national debate on Islam's place in secular France. Even before the national discussion took place, Sarkozy was offering a list to journalists of things that France definitely did not want: halal food options in school canteens, prayers outside mosques, veils, definitely *non*—and oh, *non* to minarets![18]

Other politicians play the "Islam card" in a more roundabout way and with qualifications to establish their bona fides. But once their speeches are decoded, much of the same anti-Muslim message breaks through. As a former head of communications at Carlton Television, the British prime minister David Cameron has emerged, in the last few months, as the past master of argument by qualification. Cameron's discourse is perfectly crafted à la English liberal, the reasonable man par excellence. In his Munich speech, for instance, he spoke approvingly of Islam as a peaceful religion and criticised the "hard right" for its "clash of civilisations" thesis, something he thoroughly rejected. But as the theme of his Munich speech was Islamist extremism, terrorism and national identity, when he argued that we have been "too cautious, frankly even fearful, to stand up to them", even in the face of the "horrors of forced marriage", there can be no doubt that "them" were Muslims. And here once again we see the redrafting of the theme of "aggressive minorities" out "to overawe and dominate the rest". But if Cameron echoes the Powellite theme of aggressive minorities dominating the rest of the nation, his delivery is studiously without Powell's emotionalism and inflammatory language.

All the political leaders purport to represent the voice of the beleaguered majority, but define the majority culture and the national identity that they are defending in different ways. In some cases, the politicians argue that the case against Muslims and immigrants (the two seem interchangeable; there doesn't, for instance, seem to be a single German Muslim in the whole of Germany, only Muslim immigrants) is made on the basis of secularism, Enlightenment values and liberalism. In other cases it is made in defence of Christianity, or the Judaeo-Christian Western tradition. In a few cases it is even made on behalf of the white majority. The choice of words, and the juxtaposition of arguments draw from a lexicon of victimhood: the majority are victimised by the minority; national identity is under threat from "alien cultures".

In Germany, where every one of these elements has been at play, it is the Christian *Leitmotif* that is emerging as the dominant note in the debate about *Leitkultur*. The fact that German culture is now defined by the Christian religion is a fact deplored by the respected philosopher Jürgen Habermas, who senses that behind this is a relapse into an "ethnic understanding of our liberal constitution". "With an arrogant appropriation of Judaism—and an incredible disregard for the fate the Jews suffered in Germany—the apologists of the *Leitkultur* now appeal to the 'Judeo-Christian tradition' which distinguishes us from foreigners," laments Habermas.[19]

Like Cameron, Angela Merkel attempted to be conciliatory in her Potsdam speech, stating that Islam was part of Germany. But she immediately cancelled that out by arguing in the next breath that Germany was defined by Christian values and that "those who do not accept this are in the wrong place here". Since Merkel's speech, several leading Bavarian politicians have made the link between German nationalism and Christianity even more forcefully. The Bavarian interior minister Joachim Herrmann, for instance, stated, "Our fundamental values are clearly grounded in the Christian-Western tradition. Germany does not want to integrate to Islam but rather to preserve its cultural identity".[20] The Bavarian minister for social affairs, Christine Haderthauer, argued for a hierarchy of religions stressing that "religious freedom must not become religious equality".[21] And at the beginning of March 2011, after a gun attack at Frankfurt airport which left two US servicemen dead, the new federal interior minister, Hans-Peter Friedrich (CSU), declared that Islam did not belong in Germany. In his first press conference as a minister, Friedrich said that while Muslims should be allowed to live in modern Germany, "to say that Islam belongs to Germany is not a fact supported by history".[22]

Another tack altogether has been taken by the German federal minister for family, youth and seniors, Kristina Schröder (CDU), who (apparently unable to grasp the essence of racism) is in charge of government policies to counter far-right extremism. In an interview with the *Bild* newspaper, which focused on the problem of Muslim youth, Schröder declared that "we are dealing with fundamentally hostile attitudes towards other groups—particularly against Germans and Christians. We need to act as decisively against this as against xenophobia".[23] Her comments came during a vigorous debate in the right wing media promoting the New Right's "reverse racism thesis", and suggesting that the biggest threat to Germany came from "hatred against Germans" or "racism against white Germans". The argument of reverse racism, with Germans as the true victims of the Muslim population, is gaining ground. A recent survey showed that 85 percent of parents in Berlin felt that white Christian children were discriminated against by

Muslim children.[24] That Schröder, the minister in charge of preventing extremism, could make recourse to the New Right reverse racism thesis is disturbing in itself. But when it happens while there is an upsurge in far-right violence and Islamophobic attacks in Berlin, one has to question whether she should be handling the brief to counter right wing extremism. Since November 2010 several mosques and cultural centres have come under repeated arson attacks. At least 13 arson attacks on residential buildings of migrants in Berlin Neukölln took place in the first three months of 2011.[25]

Nativism, jobs and benefits

The fact that mainstream politicians are now speaking to the fear and hatred promoted by the extreme-right's anti-multicultural platform, and thereby legitimating conspiracy theories about Muslims, is not lost on the extreme-right. As an excited Geert Wilders told the *Spiegel* news magazine, both Merkel and the CDU have taken "the lead in the domain of Islam criticism".[26] The FN's Marine Le Pen told the *Financial Times* that David Cameron's attack on the failures of multiculturalism is "exactly" the "type of statement that has barred us from public life for 30 years. I sense an evolution at European level, even in classic governments. I can only congratulate him".[27]

In most cases, centre-right politicians frame their attack on multiculturalism in terms of a need to dismantle barriers to integration or even, in the case of Søren Pind, assimilation. They steer clear of the extreme-right's inflammatory rhetoric, with its undertone of cultural cleansing. But this is not always the case. Nicolas Sarkozy rarely fails to reach for incendiary vocabulary. But his repeated attempts to rally FN voters often rebound on his own party. Thus in March 2011 Sarkozy had to sack his diversity adviser Abderrahmane Dahmane after Dahmane called on all Muslim members of the UMP to withhold party membership unless the national debate on Islam and secularism was cancelled. In fact Sarkozy's wish-list—no Muslims praying outside, no halal meat options in schools, and no minarets—is merely a pale reflection of the FN's programme, as UMP members well know. In December 2010 Marine Le Pen compared Muslims praying in the street outside the overcrowded mosques of certain Parisian neighbourhoods to the Nazi occupation and described 15 areas of France where Muslims so worshipped as occupied territories.[28] And the FN has launched its own programme against halal products, claiming that the majority of meat sold in supermarkets is halal, but the consumer is not being informed, even suggesting that eating such meat could somehow lead to the conversion of non-Muslims![29]

But all those politicians who single out the multicultural society as a threat to national identity also speak to the agenda of national preference that has always been central to the extreme-right. Just as Powell's attacks on immigration led to the closing of the door to primary immigration from the New Commonwealth through the immigration acts of 1968 and 1971, today's attacks on multiculturalism have brought in their wake a round of policy proposals aimed not just at Europe's Muslim communities, but also at residents, Third Country Nationals, migrant workers and new arrivals. Islamophobia is the route politicians have travelled in order to introduce new legislation to deny migrant workers access to public services, potentially exclude long-settled immigrants from a range of social benefits, and establish a policy of national preference (nativism) in employment. In this sense, it is true to say that Islamophobia and anti-Muslim racism today also serve an economic purpose.

Merkel in her Potsdam speech did not just attack multiculturalism. She also, crucially, declared that immigrant workers should not be considered for jobs "until we have done all we can to help our own people to become qualified and give them a chance".[30] National governments used to guarantee their citizens full employment, but no one speaks of full employment any more. As unemployment soars and employment rights are rescinded, as governments attack pension rights and the rights to sickness benefits, the discussion on employment resolves around the threat to "native workers" posed by foreign workers. How can we discriminate against foreign workers, or in the words of former British prime minister Gordon Brown, protect "British jobs for British workers"? Already in Denmark in July 2010 Karsten Lauritzen, integration spokesman for the ruling Liberal Party (Venstre), suggested paying immigrants half the current minimum wage. Even some in his party were horrified, and other politicians argued this would stigmatise immigrants and lead to hostility as they would be seen to undercut the wages of Danish workers.[31] And in the Netherlands, where there has been a poisonous debate on migrants from Eastern Europe, most of whom are on short-term contracts via employment agencies, Marnix Norder, the Hague City Council member in charge of integration policies (Labour Party, PvDA), published a policy paper in November 2010 advocating that the "tsunami" of Eastern European migrants be sent home. Of course he had "nothing against them individually, but there are so many".[32]

The centre-right is establishing a narrative, with some centre-left parties following suit, to justify the biggest round of public spending cuts since the 1920s, blaming the current economic crisis not on the bankers and the global financial crisis, but on immigration. Witness David Cameron's address to party members in Hampshire on 14 April. Though drawing from his usual bag of caveats, Cameron, with a nod to Powell, blamed New Labour for presiding over "the largest influx of people Britain has ever had", adding that "mass immigration" had placed "pressures on communities up and down the country", "on schools, housing and healthcare".[33] The coalition agreement of the Dutch Liberal and Christian Democrat parties, and its junior partner, Geert Wilders' Freedom Party, on coming to power in September 2010, included five pages of proposals aimed at "a substantial reduction of immigration". Soon Wilders was warning the coalition that there would be trouble ahead if immigration from "non-Western countries" was not reduced by 50 percent. Only the amendment of five EU directives and four European Treaties could realise Wilders's dream, according to Professor Cees Groenendijk, an expert on national and EU law.[34] But the coalition government's riposte (to keep Wilders quiet) is to exclude certain groups from public services, establishing thereby, a system whereby new migrants are taxed but denied access to key services. It is an approach being perfected in Denmark where the Danish People's Party, in return for propping up the Liberal-Conservative coalition, has established a stranglehold on immigration policy. There has been a long debate in Denmark about the cost of immigration in which the DPP has created the fiction that non-Western immigrants take more out in benefits than what they contribute in taxes and national insurance payments. Following the establishment of a cross-party committee to investigate foreigners' rights to public services, the Danish government outlined 28 proposals in April 2011—all of which are targeted at foreigners—to ease the pressure on the welfare state. Migrants will have to earn their right to healthcare and social services, but will still have to pay taxes. Other proposals include: mandatory private health insurance for foreigners in their first four years in the country; foreigners having to pay to visit the doctor in their first two years; extending the required residency of foreigners to qualify for housing subsidies; reduced childcare benefits in the first two years.[35] The government has also proposed a change to pension rules for refugees, establishing a requirement that they have lived in Denmark for 40 years before they qualify for a full pension.

Language as nation

A recurring theme in the debates about multiculturalism and national identity and immigrants and Muslims causing the economic crisis is the issue of language or, more accurately, "language deficit". Government hypocrisy is at its most blatant when immigrants are blamed for not learning the language when the self-same government slashes funding for language provision. As the Austrian cabinet approved new pre-entry integration language requirements, and the Social Democrat and Conservative coalition government considered new legislation which would lead to the deportation of immigrants whose German does not reach a certain level in the first few years of living in the country, the Green Party spokesperson for integration in Vienna, Alev Korun, warned, "The German language is increasingly being used as a marginalisation tool".[36] David Cameron, in his Hampshire speech, even went so far as to blame those who fail to learn the language for the breakdown in neighbourhood connectedness stating that "real communities" are bound together by "common experiences...forged by friendship and conversation" so that when "significant numbers of new people" arrive in neighbourhoods "perhaps not able to speak the language", neighbourhoods become more "disjointed". In an interview with the *Guardian*, German finance minister Wolfgang Schauble (CDU) underlined his belief that it had been a mistake to recruit so many guest workers from Turkey during the economic boom of the 1960s. He claimed that he now found that some people were living in Germany who do not speak the language.[37] (It is worth noting that in times of full employment and when countries such as the Netherlands and Germany relied on foreign workers from Turkey and North Africa, the fact they did not speak Dutch or German never seemed to cause a problem.) At the October 2010 party conference in Munich the CSU adopted a seven-point plan which included sanctions against those immigrants who could not speak fluent German. Proposals in other European countries are also based on sanctions for a so-called language deficit.

A new word has been coined in German: *Integrationsverweigerer* (literally integration refuser). It is used to describe those immigrants who show a lack of willingness to adapt, for instance, by failing to attend German language classes. The language issue is so potent for those who want to revive German nationalism that the right wing *Bild* has backed an initiative by the Association for the German Language and the Association for German Cultural Relations to change the German Constitution so that the primacy of the German language is acknowledged. The paper is encouraging its readers to send letters to the Association for the German Language stating, "I don't want third generation immigrant families who refuse to learn the language of the country they live in." The fight to defend cultural, religious and civil rights in Europe—which currently centres around the veil, mosques and minarets—may have to extend to include a fight to preserve minority languages. Cameron's observation that "real communities" are forged by "friendship and conversation" can easily morph—as indeed it already has in Berlin and, in the past, in Rotterdam—into an administrative instruction that no foreign languages be spoken in the playground or in public spaces. Kenan Kolat, chair of the Turkish Community in Germany, clearly saw such regressive thinking as a distinct possibility when he warned that if the German constitution were indeed changed there had to be a sub-clause to the effect that, "The state must respect the identity of cultural and linguistic minorities".[38]

◆ Thanks to Sibille Merz for research on Germany.

◆ A version of this essay appeared on the IRR website, posted on 21 April 2011 http://www.irr.org.uk/2011/april/ha000021.html. The editor thanks the author and the Institute of Race Relations for kindly granting permission for the article to be reproduced in this collection.

The freedom to express who we are

ZITA HOLBOURNE

Multiculturalism is many things to many people but one thing it most definitely is not is a government policy. Multiculturalism is about respecting, celebrating, sharing and honouring our many traditions, cultures, languages, religions, non-religion, histories and lifestyles. Multiculturalism is sometimes seen as a celebration of diversity, but it's much more than that.

It's about having the freedom to express who we are without fear of repercussions if we do, and about celebrating who we are. It cannot be defined with one phrase and it can't be limited to a definition decided by a politician. Multiculturalism is more powerful than the government of the day—it's about who we are, where we come from and where we are going, and no politician can take that away.

It's what makes us a strong, vibrant and enriched society. It's about self-definition and self-determination and it helps us to have the confidence to share and embrace our traditions and uniqueness. Multiculturalism is ever-changing and ever evolving as we embrace traditions that are ancient, handed down to us through generations while adopting, adapting and experiencing new ones so the two fuse together to create an eclectic explosion of religion, culture, music, food, language and lifestyle.

Why should we defend it?

So why should we defend multiculturalism? If you take away multiculturalism, which you could never do anyway, you take away the very essence of what makes us who we are and what makes the UK the country it is. You take away our strength and our unity. In order to take away multiculturalism you would have to erase history—centuries of enslavement, invasion and migration.

David Cameron is trying to link multiculturalism to extremism. This is dangerous and irresponsible. In effect it is racist and Mr Cameron as leader of the government has a responsibility to promote harmony between different races and religions and a duty of care towards all citizens, not just a chosen few that he feels he can relate to. The aspects of multiculturalism he does not like are not the aspects embraced by the upper class Oxbridge-educated millionaire circles he moves in but the aspects embraced by working class black and Asian people. His attack on multiculturalism is a direct attack on certain faiths, specifically Islam, and on race equality. David Cameron wants to strip us of our right to celebrate and embrace who we are as individuals, as communities and as UK citizens, but only some of us—he's not suggesting his Eton-educated chums branch out and make new friends or that Sloane Rangers come down to the East End and hang out with the locals in the Boleyn pub. His comments were directed at specific sections of the population and he has expressed negative and wrong perceptions about those sections.

This is not the first time that he has attacked multiculturalism. In a debate hosted by the Equality and Human Rights Commission in 2008, Cameron defined "state multiculturalism" as the idea that we should respect different cultures within Britain to the point of allowing them and encouraging them to live separate lives, apart from each other and apart from the mainstream. So in effect stating in 2011 that "state multiculturalism" has not worked he is saying that we should disrespect different cultures, not allow them to live separate lives, and that we should all live together. Cameron therefore seems to be advocating for communes for clones and for people to discriminate against each other. It would seem that the attack on multiculturalism is likely to rear its head again and this is why it is important that we counter the negative and dangerous comments about it that do nothing to promote equality and are more likely to provide ammunition for the far right to use towards black and Asian people.

As a second generation black woman of mixed race heritage there are many aspects to my culture, and while it is impossible for me to stop embracing my multiculturalism, if it were possible I would refuse. It was a long and painful journey for me to understand and deal with the racism I faced growing up, to not just accept but grow to like and be proud of the person I was, to shake off several layers of negative assumptions and prejudice towards me because of how I looked, my black heritage, my mixed heritage, the cultural traditions I embraced. Promotion of multiculturalism is one of the ways I was able to do this because through multiculturalism came an acceptance of different cultures and our right to be. While once I had kept quiet about those traditions in the company of those I didn't know well, even trying to conform sometimes to a fake "norm", I became not only emboldened but delighted in both owning my cultural traditions in public and sharing them. My multiculturalism is where I draw my strength and confidence from. Muhammad Ali said, "I am American. I am the part you won't recognise. But get used to me. Black, confident, cocky, my name, not yours, my religion, not yours, my goals, my own, get used to me."

Embracing my culture and traditions manifests in all aspects of my life. As a poet, as a visual artist, as a trade union representative and a community activist it plays a key part. My life path has been influenced not just by my own culture but the cultures I have experienced throughout my life both in the UK and other countries. I am fortunate to have friends and family in many different parts of the world and travelling to a range of countries across four continents has afforded me the opportunity to observe, learn from and identify with many different cultures, religions and traditions which have in turn enriched my life experience. Within my family there are English, Welsh, Irish, Trinidadian, Venezuelan, St Lucian, Barbadian, American, Canadian, Colombian, Spanish, French, Sri Lankan, Native American, Italian and Gibraltarian members observing five different religions or none at all.

In the UK I have friends and colleagues who are many different religions and ethnicities and these, along with the family members, mean my life experience is more interesting and exciting as a result of us all sharing the cultural traditions we embrace.

It is because of multiculturalism that we are enriched and stronger as a society. It's for these reasons and many more that it is essential for us to defend multiculturalism.

The key role of the trade union movement

As a trade union representative I am very committed to combating discrimination and achieving equality. In fact it was my interest in equality and justice that led me to become a trade union representative. I believe there is a strong link between equality and multiculturalism because both are positive forces in challenging discrimination.

The trade union movement has a key role to play in defence of multiculturalism. Trade unions, just like employers and service providers, have a legal and moral duty to promote good relations between people of different races, colours, ethnicities, religions and cultures.

Equality is supposed to be at the heart of everything a trade union does, and tackling discrimination while promoting and practicing equality is an integral part of every campaign and policy it has. Embracing multiculturalism is a positive way of promoting equality.

While multiculturalism is being attacked by the far right and linked to race and religion in a negative way, defending it needs to be embedded in anti-racist and anti-fascist activities and campaigns by unions and activists and within equality policies and initiatives.

Because there are different understandings of what multiculturalism means, including the bizarre definition of "state multiculturalism" Mr Cameron talks about , it's important that dialogue takes place in the first instance within the union movement at all levels about what multiculturalism both represents to the trade union movement and means to different people, because you can't have a collective defence of something that is not understood by those who are defending it, and without that dialogue there is potential for division caused through misunderstanding. If unions include multiculturalism in their equality and anti-racist/anti-fascist work this gives an opportunity to discuss, define and defend. Alongside this an awareness of and understanding of different religions is important, particularly Islam, given the rise of Islamaphobia and Cameron's linking of multiculturalism with extremism.

The TUC and all trade unions have equality policies and multiculturalism can be included in those policies and anti-racist/anti-fascist policies. There are charters for equality and a charter in defence of multiculturalism could be drawn up at TUC level that could be signed up to by trade union leaders giving a commitment at top level to its defence. This top level commitment should not be instead of anything else but in addition to gaining the same kind of commitment from individual trade unions and from equality structures within them. Unions could write model motions in defence of multiculturalism to aid the debate but also so that it becomes part of union policy. Workshops and discussion forums could be facilitated and organised. It is important that these involve anti-racist organisations, faith groups, black community organisations and those on the receiving end of prejudice and discrimination linked to attacks on multiculturalism.

My trade union, the Public and Commercial Services union (PCS), has already started the process of forming policy and awareness. My union provided some awareness sessions on main religions a few years ago. In April 2011 PCS submitted an emergency motion to the TUC Black Workers Conference entitled "Condemn David Cameron's attack on multiculturalism", which I moved and the Communication Workers Union seconded, as follows:

◆ Conference notes that David Cameron's speech at the Munich Security Meeting (5 February 2011) claimed multiculturalism had failed the UK and referred to extremist/terrorist incidents to justify the false claim.
◆ Conference is concerned by Cameron's speech on the same day EDL extremists besieged Luton to vent fascist/anti-Islamic poison. Yet he chose not to condemn EDL extremism.
◆ Conference agrees that Cameron should focus on sorting out the economic mess caused by financial institutions; investing in Britain's future, not stoking disharmony across Europe by denouncing multiculturalism. Conference condemns Cameron for playing the hate-mongering "trump" immigration card.
◆ Conference agrees the TUC Race Committee
   — should seek the signatures of all affiliated members, general secretaries and others, to challenge the attack on multiculturalism

— encourage all affiliates to actively affiliate to, support and promote the "One Society, Many Cultures" campaign to showcase the positive contributions that Black people and multiculturalism continue to make to Britain

— demand an explanation from Mr Cameron as to why he chose to conflate multiculturalism with extremism and

— ask David Cameron to outline how he will tackle extremist elements within groups like the EDL and BNP.

The motion was carried unanimously, which means that it is now union policy to carry out the instructions in the motion.

Key things trade unions can do to kick start the process

◆ Union equality committees to put defence of multiculturalism and combating islamophobia on their agendas and initiate discussion.

◆ Draw up model motions defending multiculturalism.

◆ Enter discussions with anti-racist/anti-fascist organisations about how we can work together.

◆ Call on the TUC to draw up a charter in defence of multiculturalism.

◆ Invite speakers to union meetings to talk about why the defence is important and relevant to trade unions.

◆ Publish articles in union journals about multiculturalism.

◆ Publish articles in union journals about different religions including Islam and/or provide fact sheets about key religions including Islam.

◆ Dispel any myths about Islam through dialogue and publications, eg fact sheets.

◆ Campaign against any attacks on Islam or other religions.

◆ Enter discussions with employers.

◆ Hold celebratory events to promote multiculturalism.

◆ Hold celebratory events on key religious dates.

◆ Hold awareness sessions on different religions including Islam.

◆ Invite religious leaders or observers which could include union reps and members to give talks on what their religion means to them.

◆ Ensure that their policies and practices take into account religious observance and practices, ie time off for religious observance/

holidays, provision of faith observance rooms, arranging meetings and events to take into account key religious dates.

We must ensure that the defence of multiculturalism is debated and agreed more widely than within union structures and among union members and taken to our workplaces and the communities we live in. Trade unions could look at the sectors they represent and agree a process of discussing attacks on multiculturalism with employers and gaining commitment from them to include multiculturalism in their policies and initiatives.

Con-Dem cuts will reduce the amount spent on equality initiatives and cultural events such as Black History Month, meaning that there is less scope for promotion of multiculturalism. The knock-on impact of public sector cuts on the voluntary sector who provide unique services to our multicultural communities will mean that funding is cut to important initiatives that promote equality and diversity and celebrate multiculturalism. As the cuts will hit the poorest and most vulnerable the hardest, many of whom are used as scapegoats by the far-right and right wing press, defending those communities goes hand in hand with defending multiculturalism.

Perhaps, therefore, in the same way as public sector organisations have a duty to assess the equality impacts of any cuts they are proposing, we should call on Mr Cameron to carry out an equality impact assessment on his plan to scrap multiculturalism? Will it have a disproportionate impact on race grounds—it most certainly will have an overwhelming negative and disproportionate impact—and as such Mr Cameron will need to reconsider his proposal or put forward his mitigation.

I believe that in the same way we tackle the discrimination of cuts towards black people, women, disabled people, LGBT people, pensioners and children we must tackle the impact of cuts on celebrating and promoting multiculturalism.

It is important that the positive messages about multiculturalism are brought to our schools, colleges and universities and multiculturalism continues to be celebrated in our schools while being debated, defended and promoted within the student movement. The National

Union of Students and education sector unions have a key role to play here.

One way to bring the message to our wider communities about why we are defending multiculturalism is to celebrate it. Unions regularly combine debate with art and culture in order to bring messages of unity, hope and equality to wider audiences; unions could hold multiculturalism seminars, concerts and socials and use these to not only defend multiculturalism but also raise funds for causes they support and campaigns they are running. Trade unions have a responsibility to challenge the government when they get things wrong and trade union leaders could write to the government setting out the arguments for defending multiculturalism. They can challenge any negative responses by the press to Cameron's comments and dispel any myths or lies.

Multiculturalism is here to stay

Multiculturalism is here to stay; the task ahead is about defending our right to embrace multiculturalism in an open way, to have dialogue about it and to celebrate it without fearing repercussions for doing so from the far right, racists and the current government. People should be free to embrace their own cultures without living in fear, we should be able to respect the differences between us while celebrating how those differences bring us together and unite us in such a way that we can be open about who we are.

We are not clones, we are not the same and that should be celebrated. Multiculturalism is not just important to us as individuals or ethnic and religious groups but as a response to racism and discrimination. Our right to recognise and enjoy multiculturalism is a human right and any threat to multiculturalism is a threat to our freedom. "To be free is not merely to cast off one's chains, but to live in a way that respects and enhances the freedom of others"—Nelson Mandela.

Multiculturalism
and integration:
struggling with confusions[1]

◆◆

TARIQ MODOOD

David Cameron's declaration that "multiculturalism is dead" has a long pedigree and is by no means confined to the right. Multiculturalism has always had its left as well as right wing critics, but the obituaries probably began in 1989 with Fay Weldon: "Our attempt at multiculturalism has failed. The Rushdie Affair demonstrates it" (Weldon 1989). Whatever our views on the novel *The Satanic Verses*, the Salman Rushdie affair crisis made it clear that the minority-majority faultline was not going to be simply about colour-racism; and that multiculturalism could not be confined to "steelbands, saris and samosas". For some liberals that meant the end of their support as angry Muslims muscled in on something that was only meant for secular "transgressives" like gays and black youth. Earlier street disturbances were hailed as "right on" politics but a passionate religious identity was too "multicultural" for many liberals.

Yet actually, political multiculturalism flourished as Labour came to accept ethno-religious communitarianism as it had previously accepted other assertive identity movements. Muslim faith schools, religious discrimination legislation, incitement to religious hatred, bringing Muslims into the networks of governance, including a religion question in the census—all of these have happened well after the original "death of multiculturalism"—indeed, some of them after 9/11 and 7/7, two other events that were meant to have killed off multiculturalism. One of the very last acts of New Labour was the passing of the Equality Act, which for the first time put the claims of the religion and belief strand on the same level as race. Initially having religious equality legislation because of an EU directive, Labour left office with legislation that went well beyond anything found in Europe (on race as well as religion).

One of the reasons that multiculturalism does not seem to die despite having its last rites continually read out by successive government ministers, like David Blunkett, Ruth Kelly and Hazel Blears, is that when you think about it there are very few policies at stake. This is clear from David Cameron's speech (Cameron 2011), which despite its emphatic rhetoric has very little policy content. Many people worry about residential segregation and inward looking communities. But these are not the result of policies and population distribution could only be achieved by, to coin a phrase, muscular illiberalism. Residential concentrations have resulted more from poverty, fear of racism, natural growth and "white flight" than self-ghettoisation. Research shows that all minorities—including Muslims—want to live in mixed neighbourhoods and ghettoes are created by those who move out. This is not "state multiculturalism" and could only be reversed by state racial and religious quotas on where people could live. Unless by "muscular liberalism" Cameron means that groups such as Sikhs, Hindus and Muslims are not to be included in the delegation of public responsibilities and resources that are the central idea of the Big Society.

It is individual or institutional choices, then, that create outcomes, multiculturalist or otherwise. Schools that choose their pupils, like faith schools, are less ethnically mixed than where pupils are allocated places by local authorities. The expansion of faith schools and indeed the Big Society concept in general in so far as it hands over resources and decision-making to neighbourhoods, communities, charities and organised religion should see the development, not the decline, of ethno-religious communitiarianism.

Unlike Cameron I call such state-community partnerships "multiculturalism" and I am in favour of them, with certain conditions. One is that it must be within a context of robust individual rights. John Stuart Mill's "harm principle": one person's freedom—whether in the name of multiculturalism or anti-multiculturalism—has to be limited when it's clear that others are being harmed. Muslim men demanding conformity from their womenfolk (eg, the wearing of modest dress) is

Reaching for racism: That speech in Munich

one example where individual rights may be squashed. Legislatures forbidding Muslim women from wearing modest clothes of their choice is an even more egregious example.

Yet society cannot be reduced to individuals and so integration must be about bringing new communities, and not just new individuals, into relations of equal respect. This means challenging racism and Islamophobia and so on, not by denying that there are groups in society but developing positive group identities and adapting customs and institutions that enable that.

Equally importantly, we have to talk up what we have in common. We cannot take for granted what we have in common but work hard to ensure all varieties of citizens see themselves in our shared conceptions of citizenship. Such citizenships are imaginatively shaped by our sense of country, about who we are, where we are coming from and where we are going—by our "national story". An out of date story alienates the new post-immigration communities, who want to be written into the story—backwards as well as forward. So multiculturalism is incomplete and one-sided without a continual remaking of national identity.

This is an aspect of multiculturalism that has been understated and so the inattentive assume that multiculturalism is all about emphasising difference and separatism. In fact it's about creating a new, ongoing "We" out of all the little, medium-sized and large platoons that make up the country.

In Britain we have made some progress on a number of fronts. In terms of everyday inter-racial and inter-ethnic mixing cities like London are quite remarkable. Yet we have have also made progress in relation to the communitarian and the national identity fronts. If this does not seem so in relation to the latter it's because of Britain's elusive, understated and misstated national identity. That goes back to the exigencies and contingencies of the Union and of running an empire and certainly predates multiculturalism. Even today ethnic minorities are more likely to say they are British than white people. It is more white reticence than minority separatism that is an obstacle to an inclusive national identity and without overcoming which multicultural nation-building is difficult.

Identifying and responding to "difference"

It will be clear from what I have said so far that there is a lot of confusion about what multiculturalism is and what it is not. This is partly because "multiculturalism" is too often defined by its critics, whose sole purpose is to create a straw man to knock down. But its also because there is more than one form of multiculturalism and they relate to integration in different ways. I would like to use the rest of my chapter to clarify the key terms of assimilation, integration, cosmopolitanism and multiculturalism.[2] I hope this helps us better to debate properly, to have a clear idea of what is being said or objected to. I would like to think that my analysis will bring people closer to my own advocacy of multiculturalism, but it will have succeeded if it increases understanding of what the issues are.

Assimilation, integration, diversity and multiculturalism each offer their own distinctive take on freedom, equality and civic unity (what might be called, "fraternity"), namely, some of the core values of European democracy. The issue or "problem" that all four of these paradigms are addressing is post-immigration "difference" (Modood 2007). Large scale immigration into Europe from outside Europe has been by people marked by "difference". The "difference" is not confined to the fact of migration, or how long the migrants and their families have been in Europe or the fact that they come from less economically developed parts of the world—namely aspects which can be stated structurally and quantitatively. "Difference" primarily refers to how people are identified: how they identify themselves (eg, as "white", "black", "Chinese", "Muslim"), how they identify others (again, as "white", "black", "Chinese", "Muslim", etc) and how they are identified by others ("white", etc). These identities fall (not necessarily unambiguously or discretely) within the fields of "race", ethnicity, religion, culture and nationality, what I will call the forms of difference. They will no doubt be classed or gendered in specific or generalisable ways but the important point from which everything else follows is that these identities are not reducible to or—stronger still—are not primarily socio-economic or "objective" in classical sociological terms. The relevant interactions cannot be explained, the position of different actors predicted or even guessed at, political preferences expressed and so on without the explicit or implicit use of the forms of difference. I take "integration" to mean the process whereby difference ceases to be problematic. I shall consider four modes of integration (summarised in Table 1).

Assimilation is where the processes affecting change and the relationship between social groups are seen as one-way, where the preferred result is one where the newcomers do little to disturb the society they are settling in and become as much like their new compatriots as possible. We may think of it as one-way integration. By smothering difference it is also thought that the occasions for discrimination and conflict are not allowed to take root. From the 1960s onwards, beginning with Anglophone countries and spreading to others, assimilation as a policy has come to be seen as impractical (especially for those who stand out in terms of physical appearance), illiberal (requiring too much state intervention) and inegalitarian (treating indigenous citizens as a norm to which others must approximate). It was as early as 1966 that Roy Jenkins, the home secretary at the time, declared that in the view of the British government integration is "not a flattening process of assimilation but equal opportunity accompanied by cultural diversity in an atmosphere of mutual tolerance" (Jenkins 1967, p267). While "assimilation" as a term has come to be dropped in favour of "integration", yet even today when some politicians use the term "integration", they actually, consciously or not, mean what here has been defined as assimilation, so the use of these terms in public discourse must not be taken at their face value but critically inspected.

Non-assimilative integration is where processes of social interaction are seen as two-way, and where members of the majority community as well as immigrants and ethnic minorities are required to do something; so the latter cannot alone be blamed for failing to or not trying to integrate. The established society is the site of institutions—including employers, civil society and the government—in which integration has to take place, and accordingly they must take the lead. The new (prospective) citizens' rights and opportunities must be made effective through anti-discrimination laws and policies. We need, however, to distinguish between *individualist-integration* and *multiculturalism*. The former sees the institutional adjustments in relation to migrants or minorities as only individual claimants and bearers of rights as equal citizens (Barry 2001). Minority communities may exist as private associations but are not recognised or supported in the public sphere.

Multiculturalism is where processes of integration are seen both as two-way and as involving groups as well as individuals and working differently for different groups (CMEB 2000; Parekh 2000; Modood 2007). In this understanding, each group is distinctive, and thus integration cannot consist of a single template (hence the "multi"). The "culturalism"—by no means a happy term either in relation to "culture" or "ism"—refers to the explicitness that the groups in question are likely not just to be marked by newness or phenotype or socioeconomic location but by certain forms of group identities. The integration of groups is in addition to, not as an alternative to, the integration of individuals, anti-discrimination measures and a robust framework of individual rights.

The concept of equality is central to multiculturalism as well as to other conceptions of integration. The key difference between individualist integration and multiculturalism is that the concepts of group and of "multi" are essential to the latter. Post-immigration minorities are groups differentiated from the majority society or the norm in society by two kinds of processes. On the one hand, by the fact of negative "difference": with alienness, inferiorisation, stigmatisation, stereotyping, exclusion, discrimination, racism and so on. On the other hand, by the senses of identity that groups so perceived have of themselves. The two together are the key data for multiculturalism. The differences at issue are those perceived both by outsiders or group members— from the outside in and from the inside out—to constitute not just some form of distinctness but a form of alienness or inferiority that diminishes or makes difficult equal membership in the wider society or polity. Multicultural accommodation of minorities, then, is different from individualist-integration because it explicitly recognises the social reality of groups, not just of individuals and organisations. There may, however, be considerable complexity about what is meant by social reality of groups or groupness here, and ideas of groups as discrete, homogeneous, unchanging, bounded populations are not realistic when we are thinking of multicultural recognition (Modood 2007, pp93-7). This leads us to cosmopolitanism.

Further unpacking multiculturalism and integration

Cosmopolitanism emerges by accepting the concept of difference while critiquing or dissolving the concept of groups (Waldron 1991).[3] Disagreement about the extent to which post-immigration groups exist and/or ought to exist and be given political status means that there are two kinds of multiculturalism (Modood 1998; Meer and Modood 2009). While in public discourse as well as in academia one or both are referred to as multiculturalism, and often without a full recognition that two different ideas are being expressed, I will reserve the term "multiculturalism" for the sociological and political position in which groups are a critical feature.[4] Where "difference" is positively valorised (or pragmatically accepted) but it is denied that groups exist or, alternatively, exist but should not be politically recognised, I shall call cosmopolitanism. The contention is that in the early stages of migration and settlement, especially in the context of a legacy of racism, colonialism and European supremacism, forms of social exclusion created or reinforced certain forms of groupness such as white and black, but as a result of social mixing, cultural sharing and globalisation in which dominant identities of modernity, such as of race and nation, are dissolving, people have much more fluid and multiple identities, combine them in individual ways and use them in context-sensitive ways (Hall 1992). For example, the ways that Caribbean-origin Britons have socially blended into a "multiculture" and have sought conviviality and sociability rather than separate communities may perhaps not be fully captured as a form of individualistic integration (Gilroy 2000). While remaining economically marginal and over-represented in relation to the social problems associated with deprived inner cities, they have become a feature of popular culture in terms of music, dance, youth styles and sport, in all of which they have become significantly over-represented (Hall 1998). To the extent that football teams, Olympiads and television programmes such as *The X Factor* are central to popular and national identities, Caribbean-origin people are placed at the centre of British national imaginaries. Moreover, Britain and most other countries in Western Europe have recently experienced and are experiencing a new wave of immigration and will continue to do

Table 1: Four modes of integration*

	Assimilation	*Individualist-Integration*	*Cosmopolitanism*	*Multiculturalism*
Objects of policy	Individuals and groups marked by "difference"	Individuals marked by "difference", especially their treatment by discriminatory practices of state and civil society	Individuals marked by "difference", especially their treatment by discriminatory practices of state and civil society, and societal ideas, especially of "us" and "them"	Individuals and groups marked by "difference", especially their treatment by discriminatory practices of state and civil society, and societal ideas, especially of "us" and "them"
Liberty	Minorities must be encouraged to conform to the dominant cultural pattern	Minorities are free to cultivate their identities in private but are discouraged from thinking of themselves as minority, but rather as individuals	Neither minority nor majority individuals should think of themselves as belonging to a single identity but be free to mix 'n match	Members of minorities should be free to assimilate, to mix 'n match or to cultivate group membership in proportions of their own choice
Equality	Presence of difference provokes discrimination and so is to be avoided	Discriminatory treatment must be actively eliminated so everyone is treated as an individual and not on the basis of difference	Anti-discrimination must be accompanied by the dethroning of the dominant culture	In addition to anti-discrimination the public sphere must accommodate the presence of new group identities and norms
Fraternity	A strong, homogeneous national identity	Absence of discrimination and nurturing of individual autonomy within a national, liberal democratic citizenship	People should be free to unite across communal and national boundaries and should think of themselves as global citizens	Citizenship and national identity must be remade to include group identities that are important to minorities as well as majorities; the relationship between groups should be dialogical rather than one of domination or uniformity.

* In all cases it is assumed that a backdrop of liberal democratic rights and values are operative to a large degree and what is highlighted here is in addition or interaction with them.

so, including from within the European Union. Given the diversity of the locations from whence migrants are coming, the result, it is argued, is not communities, but a churning mass of languages, ethnicities and religions, all cutting across each other and creating a "superdiversity" (Vertovec 2007). This may be setting a pattern for the future, and it may be allied to a further argument that globalisation, migration and telecommunications have created populations dispersed across countries that interact more with each other, and have a greater sense of loyalty to each other, than they might to their fellow citizens.

In what ways does cosmopolitanism go beyond individualist-integration? Primarily not as a politics but as an ethos: we should value diversity and create the conditions where it is individually chosen. We should oppose all forms of imposition of group identities on individuals and therefore the social imaginaries and prejudices by which individuals are inferiorised or portrayed as threatening and so excluded from full membership of society. Nor should we require assimilation or conformity to dominant group norms; yet a requirement of communal membership can also be oppressive of individuals and their life chances (Appiah 1994). Inherited or ascribed identities—such as black or Muslim—which slot people into pigeonholes not of their choosing, giving them a script to live by should be refused (often referred to in the literature as a transgression of boundaries). They not only reduce the options of the kind of person one can be but divide society up into antagonistic groups.[5] The conception is of multiculturalism as maximum freedom, for minority as well as majority individuals, to mix with, borrow and learn from all (whether they are of your group or not) so individual identities are personal amalgams of bits from various groups and heritages and there is no one dominant social identity to which all must conform. The result will be a society composed of a blend of cultures, a multiculture.

While this is an attractive image of contemporary society and blends easily with the ideas of liberal democracy, it has only a partial fit with even, say, London today, let alone many parts of Britain and continental Europe. In some towns and cities, say in northern England, there is not a diversity of groups but often just two (eg, Asian Muslims and whites) and minority individuals do not float across identities, mixing and matching, but have a strong attachment to a particular identity. For example, most British Muslims seem to think of themselves in terms of "Muslim" and/or "British" (Modood 2007: p108). The fact of superdiversity is emerging alongside rather than displacing the fact of settled, especially postcolonial, communities, who have a particular historical relationship with Britain, and the political significance of such communities. Similarly, there are other communities in other European countries with their own historical significance, such as Maghrebians in France and the Turks in Germany. Moreover, some groups continue to be much larger than others, and stand out as groups—in their own eyes and those of others—and are at the centre of public policy and debate, especially if they are thought to be failing to integrate. Muslims, for example, seem to be in this category across much of Western Europe regardless of the degree of conviviality or superdiversity that might be present. Which is not to say that such minority identities are exclusive. Successive surveys have shown that most Muslims in Britain strongly identify with being Muslim but the majority also identify as British, indeed are more likely to identify with "British" and say they have trust in key British institutions than non-Muslims (Heath and Roberts 2008; Gallup 2009 found the same in Germany, albeit less so in France though Pew 2006 found much higher levels of national identification in France than other Western European countries). Post-immigration hyphenated identities, such as British-Indian, have become as commonplace in Britain as they have been in the US for decades. Similarly, diasporic links as described above certainly exist, and are likely to increase, but I am unconvinced that the net result is an inevitable erosion of national citizenship: British African-Caribbeans and South Asians have families in their countries of origin and in the US and Canada, but there is little evidence that most branches of those families do not feel British, American, Canadian, etc.

An important point of difference, then, between the concepts of individualist-integration and multiculturalism proper is that for the latter, the groups in question, the post-immigration minorities, are not of one kind but are a "multi". For example, some people will identify with a "colour" identity like "black" but there will be others for whom national origin identities (like Turkish), or a regional heritage (like Berber), or a religious identity (like Sikh) may be much more meaningful, expressing forms of community and ethnic pride that are struggling for recognition and inclusion. And of course these minority identities will interact with wider, societal identities—woman, working class, Londoner, British—in differing ways, expressing the different experiences, locations and aspirations of different groups. So both the alternative models of multiculturalism as cosmopolitanism and as ethno-religious communitarianism have some grounding and meet the political aspirations of some minority groups. Neither works as a comprehensive sociological or political model and should be viewed as complementary (Modood 1998; CMEB 2000; Modood and Dobbernack 2011). Moreover, while recognition of ethnic or religious groups may have a legal dimension, for the most part it will be at the level of civic consultations, political participation, institutional policies (for example, schools and hospitals), discursive representations, especially in relation to the changing discourses of societal unity or national identity and their remaking. Regardless of the extent to which recognition of minority identities in this way is formal or informal, led by the state or the semi-autonomous institutions of civil society, it does not challenge, let alone displace, individual rights and the shared dimensions of citizenship. There may however be genuine concern that some groups at a particular time and in some areas are becoming too inward looking; where the concern is primarily about a lack of positive mixing and interaction between groups at a local level, community cohesion measures may be an appropriate response (Cantle 2001), and where the concern is about self-conceptions and discourses more generally, the issue will be about the national or societal identity.

Ways in which multiculturalism is not dead

This unpacking of what I mean by "multiculturalism" is also helpful in understanding those who say that multiculturalism has failed or that multiculturalism is dead. They may mean to endorse assimilation, individualistic integration or cosmopolitanism. At the same time they are acknowledging and possibly reinforcing the sociological reality of group difference because their lament is that some groups (especially Muslims) are clearly visible as distinct groups when they should not be (they attribute this fact to a separatist tendency in the groups, encouraged by allegedly "multiculturalist" policies). Hence, paradoxical as it may sound, fierce critics of multiculturalism are usually deploying the sociology of multiculturalism even while rejecting its political dimensions. If they thought these groups were merely the product of stereotypes and exclusion (in the sense that "racial" groups are a product of racism) or were primarily socio-economic in character (perhaps a working class "fraction"), then that would be a sociological disagreement with the multiculturalists. The irony is of course that the accusatory discourse of "some groups are not integrating" may actually be reinforcing group identities and therefore contributing to the social conditions that gives multiculturalism a sociological pertinence. On the other hand, a sociology that marginalised ethnicity in favour of say, individuals, class and gender, would have a better fit with anti-multiculturalist politics but may be unable to explain or predict the relevant social reality.

Moreover, it is not just at the level of sociology that anti-multiculturalists may find themselves using multiculturalist ideas; even while deploying an anti-multiculturalist discourse they may enact multiculturalist policies. For example, they may continue with group consultations, representation and accommodation. The latter have actually increased. The British government has found it necessary to increase the scale and level of consultations with Muslims in Britain since 9/11, and, dissatisfied with existing organisations, has sought to increase the number of organised interlocutors and the channels of communication. Avowedly anti-multiculturalist countries and governments have worked to increase corporatism in practice, for example with the creation by Nicholas Sarkozy of the *Conseil Francais du Culte Musulman* in 2003 to represent all Muslims to the French government in matters of worship and ritual; and by the creation of the *Islamkonferenz* in Germany in 2005, an exploratory body, yet with an extensive political agenda. These bodies are partly top-down efforts to control Muslims or to channel them into certain formations and away from others; nevertheless, such institutional processes cannot be understood within the conceptual framework of assimilation, individualist integration or cosmopolitanism. There is indeed a new intolerance in relation to certain Muslim practices (eg, the burqa) and this is leading to some new laws or policies in parts of Europe (though not yet in Britain). The point is that we do not seem to be witnessing a shift in models, for example, from pluralistic integration to individualist integration.

This analytical framework helps us also to understand those who say they welcome diversity but seem to be in agreement with critics of multiculturalism. Critics of multiculturalism are usually pointing to the public assertion of strong group identities to mobilise a group to achieve certain policies and/or to demand differential treatment. They are sometimes responded to by those who point to how multiculturalism is working in their neighbourhoods, which they say are multi-ethnic and where people do not just live peaceably side by side but mix freely and where that mixing is valued above monoculturalism. Yet such views do not imply support for strong group identities and related policies; on the contrary, their success may be seen to be dependent on the absence of the latter.[6] While this is a reasonable response in its own terms it does not meet the criticism of multiculturalism and in fact may share it. Group-based multiculturalism has become unpopular and is what critics have in mind; though this is obscured by the fact that what I call "cosmopolitanism" is often referred to by its advocates as "multiculturalism". For example, it has been argued that the majority of Australians welcome "multiculturalism", indeed they see it as part of the country's identity but they see it "in terms of a mix of individuals rather than an ensemble of groups" (Brett and Moran 2011, p203; for a related discussion in relation to England, see Fenton and Mann 2011). A group-based multiculturalism is much less popular than cosmopolitanism, but what we have to consider is whether integration of all post-immigration formations can be achieved without the latter (Modood 1998; 2007)? Moreover, a group-based multiculturalism, where group membership is voluntary, may be part of the future in an unintended way: it is highly compatible with prime minister Cameron's vision of a "Big Society" in which civil society associations based on locality and faith, including interfaith groups, take over some responsibilities currently undertaken by state agencies. If it is the case that groups such as Muslims are to be civil society partners of government, and to be delegated resources as such, it is difficult to see how the new "Big Society" is a break with what is rejected as "state multiculturalism".

Finally, moving beyond a focus on exclusion and minorities is a third level of multiculturalism, which is not just about sociology (the first level) or politics (second level), but a positive vision of the whole remade so as to include the previously excluded or marginalised on the basis of equality and sense of belonging. It is at this level that we may fully speak of multicultural integration or multicultural citizenship (Taylor 1994; Parekh 2000; Modood 2007). This third level of multiculturalism, incorporating the sociological fact of diversity, groupness and exclusion but going beyond individual rights and political accommodation, is perhaps the level that has been least emphasised. Or at least that is how it seems to many whose understanding of multiculturalism, sometimes polemical but sometimes sincere, is that multiculturalism is about encouraging minority difference without a counterbalancing emphasis on cross-cutting commonalities and a vision of a greater good. This has led many commentators and politicians to talk of multiculturalism as divisive and productive of segregation. Theorists of multiculturalism such as Taylor (1994) and Parekh (2000), related policy documents such as the *Report of the Commission the Future of Multi-Ethnic Britain* (CMEB 2000) and enactments such as those in Canada and Australia, universally regarded as pioneers and exemplars of state multiculturalism, all appealed to and built on an idea of national citizenship. Hence, from a multiculturalist point of view, though not from that of its critics, the recent emphasis on cohesion and citizenship, what has been called "the civic turn" (Mouritsen 2008), is a necessary re-balancing of the political multiculturalism of the 1990s, which largely took the form of accommodation of groups while being ambivalent about national identity (Meer and Modood 2009a). This does not invalidate the analysis offered here that integration without some degree of institutional accommodation is unlikely to be successful. Indeed, for multiculturalists a renewing of national identity has to be distinctly plural and hospitable to the minority identities. It involves "rethinking the national story" with the minorities as important characters; not obscuring difference but weaving it into a common identity that all can see themselves in and giving all a sense of belonging to each other (CMEB 2000, pp54-56; Modood 2007, pp145-154). Minority politics are common in the US but most groups, while honouring their origins, seek inclusion in the American dream. They seek to be and have come to be accepted as hyphenated Americans (Italian-Americans, Asian-Americans, etc) and the trend is present in parts of Western Europe and, while not yet fully accepted, it may be that hyphenated nationalities will become the norm here too.

Conclusion

It may be the case that all the attempted models of integration, not just in Britain but across Europe, are in crisis. We can however have a better sense of what the issues are and so what needs to be done if, firstly, we recognise that discourses of integration and multiculturalism are exercises in conceptualising post-immigration difference and as such operate at three distinct levels: as an (implicit) sociology; as a political response; and as a vision of what is the whole in which difference is to be integrated. Depending upon the sociology in question certain political responses are possible or not, more reasonable or less. The sociological and political assumptions are thus mutually dependent. Secondly, I have offered a framework in which four distinct political responses—assimilation, individualist-integration, cosmopolitanism and multiculturalism—illuminate each other and where each successive position attempts to include what is thought to be missing from the predecessor. Each position, however, has its merits and may be appropriate in certain contexts, depending on the sociological reading of the context. Each can be seen to be an interpretation of the classical democratic values of liberty, equality and fraternity, though not each is equally satisfactory. Each has a particular conception of equal citizenship but the value of each can only be realised if it is not imposed but is the preferred choice of minority individuals and groups, who of course—being a "multi"—are bound to choose differently. Thus no singular model is likely to be suitable for all groups. To have a reasonable chance of integrating the maximum number of members of minorities, none of these political responses should be dismissed.

Ethno-religious communitarianism may currently be viewed as undesirable by European publics and policymakers but given how central Muslims have become to the prospects of integration on a number of fronts, it is unlikely that integration can be achieved without some element of this approach, which is being practised even by those politicians who are making anti-multiculturalist speeches. Perceptions of Muslims as groups, by themselves and by non-Muslim majorities, are hardening; so the key question is whether they are to be stigmatised as outsiders or recognised as integral to the polity. Finally, we must not overlook the third analytical level, which in many ways is not primarily about minorities but about the majority. The enlargement, hyphenation and internal pluralising of national identities is essential to an integration in which all citizens have not just rights but a sense of belonging to the whole as well as to their own "little platoon".

One Society
Many Cultures

◆◆

SABBY DHALU

One of the most concerning developments in international political and social relations over the last decade has been the dramatic rise of Islamophobia and racism directed against Muslim communities. Furious international debates have been raging over the last few years about Muslim women's right to wear religious dress, scare stories about halal meat, threats to burn the Quran, bans on minarets, offensive cartoons of the Prophet Mohammed and acts of terrorism committed by minority sections of the Muslim community used to negatively portray Islam and over one billion Muslim people around the world. Islamophobia has provided the cutting edge of the growth in support for far-right and fascist organisations across Europe.

Prime minister David Cameron launched a political attack on multiculturalism and Britain's Muslim communities, while failing to condemn the English Defence League (EDL) on the day of one of their largest demonstrations. Over the last two years the EDL has been demonstrating against Muslim communities and mosques, reminiscent of the National Front demonstrations against black, Asian and immigrant communities in the 1970s. Even the Labour Party has not been immune to Islamophobia, as the actions of Phil Woolas, former Labour MP for Oldham East and Saddleworth, show. Woolas lost his seat and was suspended from the Labour Party after falsely suggesting that a rival candidate was courting Muslim extremists during the 2010 general election campaign.

As Europe demonstrates, the growth of Islamophobia in particular is a serious social and political problem and must be combated. One

Society Many Cultures is a new national campaign formed to combat the rise of Islamophobia and all manifestations of racism, to defend freedom of thought, conscience, religion and cultural expression, and demonstrate the enormous contribution of our multicultural society to Britain's economy and culture.

Bans on niqabs and burkas and Islamophobia in Europe

A Europe-wide campaign against a Muslim woman's right to wear the niqab and burka (face and full body veil) is advancing. In France legislation banning "face coverings" came into force on 11 April 2011. It is now illegal to wear garments such as the niqab or burka, which incorporate a full-face veil, anywhere in public. Women who break the law face fines of 150 euros (£119) with 30,000 euros and a one-year jail term for men who force their wives to wear the Burka.[1] Similar legislation was passed in the lower house of the Belgian parliament in April 2010, where those who break the law face a fine of 15 to 25 euros (£13 to £27) or a seven-day jail sentence.[2] In June 2010 the mayor of Barcelona, Jordi Hereu, announced a ban on the niqab in municipal offices, public markets and libraries, but not the streets.[3] Last year a referendum in Switzerland voted in favour of banning the construction of minarets.

The experience in France since the enforcement of the ban on the niqab shows that this legislation is unworkable. Manuel Roux, deputy head of a union representing local police chiefs, in an interview with France Inter radio said the ban would be difficult to enforce, especially if Muslim women wearing a face veil refuse to remove their veil, and are surrounded by Muslim men. This could get the police involved in unnecessary altercations when there are serious crimes that need to be addressed. Secondly, many Muslim women have said they will defy the law, continue to wear the veil and simply pay the fine. A businessman has offered to sell a property worth 2 million euros in order to fund the payment of fines for women who refuse to remove the face veil. Therefore this law is unlikely to prevent Muslim women from wearing the face veil. More likely consequences of this legislation will be racist attacks on veiled Muslim women and the growth of the far-right and fascist organisations.

Fertile ground for far-right and fascist organisations across Europe

The growth of Islamophobia has provided fertile ground for the far-right and fascist organisations, the most notable example being the Front National in France. During the last three years President Sarkozy's attacks on Muslim communities have had the effect of resurrecting the Front National (FN). In the 2007 presidential elections the FN's vote fell dramatically to 4.3 percent compared to the vote it received in 2002, when Le Pen pushed the Socialist Party's Lionel Jospin into second place. However, in the 2011 regional elections the FN received 15 percent (36 percent in the constituencies where it stood candidates), a massive increase from the 6.8 percent the FN mustered in the European elections in 2009. There have been similar patterns in other European countries, where Islamophobia is feeding into electoral victories for the extreme right. In the general election in the Netherlands in 2010 Geert Wilders' PVV polled 15.5 percent, giving it 24 seats. In Switzerland the far-right SVP/UDC was the largest party in the October 2007 elections.

Britain and the rise of Islamophobia

Although legislation banning niqabs, burkas or minarets has not been proposed in Britain, there are worrying signs of increasing Islamophobia in British society. All mainstream political parties oppose legislation banning the burka or niqab, but prior to the 2010 general election the UK Independence Party (UKIP) and the BNP included a ban on the burka in their election manifestos, and both far-right parties polled a combined 1.5 million votes in the general election.

Following the vote in France a discussion continued for weeks in Britain about whether the burka or niqab should be banned in Britain. The immigration minister, Damian Green, described such a move as "un-British". However, Phillip Hollobone, MP for Kettering, introduced a Private Members Bill banning the burka, and has said that he would refuse to speak to a constituent wearing the niqab visiting his surgery. The human rights organisation Liberty announced it would represent any of his constituents that Hollobone refuses to meet and warned him that the UK's Equality Act and the European Convention on Human Rights (ECHR) oblige him to avoid discrimination, and because his ban would only affect Muslim women it would also amount to indirect sex discrimination. Hollobone's bill did not gain sufficient support among MPs and Lords to get discussed, let alone win a vote in parliament, and the government has already spoken out against it. However, the very fact that an MP is introducing such a bill is an indicator of growing Islamophobia in Britain.

This situation is also reflected in recent opinion polls. A YouGov poll for Channel 5 showed that 67 percent of respondents surveyed were in favour of banning the full face veil in Britain.[4] More concerning is an opinion poll that coincided with the launch of the "Inspired by Muhammad"[5] advertising campaign, commissioned by the Exploring Islam Foundation,[6] that showed that 58 percent said they associated Islam with extremism, and half of those polled linked the religion with terrorism.

Freedom of thought, conscience, religion and cultural expression under attack

This Islamophobia must be vigorously opposed. It is a grotesque attack on freedom of thought, conscience, religion and cultural expression. Views once considered extreme or racist are now becoming more widespread and legitimising groups like the BNP and the EDL, and their European counterparts. Furthermore, they have provided a framework for broader attacks on basic rights, impacting on other visual religious symbols such as the Sikh turban and kara (religious bangle) or Christians wearing the cross.

The ideological justification for bans on the burka is that it is "liberating" Muslim women from men who force them to cover up. In reality, the majority of women who wear this religious dress choose to do so, and many have been interviewed by international press and media saying so. The bans are an attack on women's freedom to choose what they wear. This goes against the classic ideas of liberalism and Enlightenment values upon which Western states were built.

The foundations of liberalism and multiculturalism were outlined in one of the most famous political essays in British history, John Stuart Mill's "On Liberty". He wrote, "The sole end for which mankind are warranted...in interfering with the liberty of action of any of their number is self-protection...the only purpose for which power can be rightfully exercised over any member of a...community, against his will, is to prevent harm to others." This liberal view is frequently paraphrased as, "You should be able to do anything you want provided it does not interfere with others."

Freedom of thought, conscience, religion and cultural expression were hard won and took hundreds of years of struggle and civil wars. Such freedoms are once again under attack and must be defended. One Society Many Cultures has been set up to campaign against Islamophobia and defends these freedoms.

The growth of the EDL and the capitulation to Islamophobia

One of the most extreme examples of the attack on such freedoms is the English Defence League (EDL). The EDL is an organised fascist movement with links to the BNP, Combat 18 and other fascist organisations. Football hooligan groups such as Casuals United are also linked to the EDL. The EDL is essentially an embryonic fascist pogrom movement, and its sole aim is to intimidate Muslim and other minority sections of the population and carry out violent attacks against them.

While Muslim communities' rights are under attack, simultaneously the BNP and the EDL's so-called right to freedom of speech and expression is being defended. Nick Griffin and others in the BNP have used numerous media appearances to attack Muslims, black and immigrant communities; even though Griffin has a conviction for incitement to racial hatred for denying the Holocaust, and the leading members of the BNP have praised Hitler and the Nazi regime in Germany. More shockingly the EDL has been allowed to "demonstrate" on the streets, even though these events have led to violent attacks on innocent communities and places of worship.

Organisations like the EDL, the BNP and UKIP have benefited the most from the rise of Islamophobia. Although the BNP suffered major electoral defeats in May 2011, it has still received more votes than any other fascist organisation in British history. UKIP and the BNP polled the fourth and fifth largest votes respectively in the 2010 general election. In the 2009 European elections UKIP polled the third highest vote and pushed Labour into fourth place. The BNP also made its first ever national political breakthrough, by gaining two MEPs.

One of the most striking consequences has been the growth of the EDL. Fascists now feel emboldened to demonstrate on Britain's streets in ways not seen since the 1970s National Front demonstrations. Extreme double standards are taking root. For two years the EDL has organised demonstrations explicitly against mosques and Muslim communities. If there were demonstrations against churches and Christian communities, or synagogues and the Jewish communities, these would quite rightly be met with widespread condemnation and anger. Unfortunately, this has not been the response in the main to the EDL.

Worse still, these demonstrations have been used by the EDL to riot and violently attack not only Muslims and mosques, but all ethnic minority communities. At demonstrations in Dudley the EDL broke through police lines and went on to attack a mosque, a gurdwara (Sikh temple) and a mandir (Hindu temple), smash windows of Asian businesses and intimidate communities. Similar events took place in Stoke, where even a police officer was violently attacked. An EDL member was sentenced to 18 months in prison following this attack. In Preston the EDL chanted "Burn down a mosque", and a week later there was a fire at a nearby mosque. This is clear incitement to violence and religious hatred, yet no action is being taken against the EDL.

Like most fascist organisations before it, the EDL is against all minority ethnic minority communities, trade unions, social democrats, socialists, communists and others, but is focusing its attack on the particular form of prejudice that chimes with attitudes encouraged in the media and by some politicians—Islamophobia.

The EDL's actions have not been reported widely in the media. Instead the media has focused its attack on Muslims and Islam. Research, such as *Muslims Under Siege* by Peter Oborne and James Jones[7] and *Islamophobia and Anti-Muslim Hate Crime* by Dr Robert Lambert,[8] shows how negative media coverage has encouraged violent attacks on Muslims and helped to give legitimacy to far-right and fascist groups.

Those that have the power are refusing to take action against the EDL. The police have powers under the Public Order Act to ban demonstrations—either marches or static assemblies—if there is a clear danger to public order and safety. The police have a wealth of evidence indicating exactly this in relation to the EDL. However, with the exception of marches in Bradford and Leicester, EDL demonstrations have not been banned.

Politicians—national and local government—have failed to instruct or apply pressure on the police to ban demonstrations, and in some cases have made concessions that the EDL has welcomed. For example, the EDL called a demonstration outside Wembley Arena where a Muslim conference was taking place, supposedly in protest against Zahir Naik, an Indian Imam. However, instead of using her powers as home secretary to instruct the police to take action against the EDL, Theresa May banned Zahir Naik from entering the country. Subsequently the EDL called off their demonstration, claiming victory. Earlier this year the previous home secretary, Alan Johnson, reversed a ban on Geert Wilders entering Britain, allowing him to present his Islamophobic film *Fitna* in the House of Lords, and then granted the EDL permission to march to parliament celebrating Wilders's entry into the country.

In a similar example, the EDL called a demonstration in Tower Hamlets supposedly against the UK Islamic conference. Tower Hamlets council were aware of the event for a while, however two weeks before the event was scheduled to take place, the council issued a statement calling for the cancellation of the conference and the venue withdrew use of its premises. The EDL called off its demonstration, again claiming victory. In reality the EDL's target was not the UK Islamic conference. It wanted to demonstrate in Tower Hamlets because it is home to the biggest concentration of Muslim communities in Britain and because it wanted to target the East London Mosque. This is indicated by the EDL's numerous impromptu visits to Whitechapel and the area surrounding the East London Mosque, which have resulted in violence against the local Muslim community.

These examples show that Islamophobia is so endemic in society that those with power are willing to impose bans on the Muslim community—when there is no danger to the public—while refusing to take the same action against fascist organisations who represent a clear danger to not just the public but even the police in some cases.

Following the BNP's breakthrough in the European elections in June 2009, in addition to the emergence of the EDL, many serious violent attacks on Muslims have occurred. These have included a gang attack, including stabbings, in November 2009 on Muslim students at City University who were leaving a prayer room; the murder in September 2009 of a Muslim pensioner, Ikram Syed ul-Haq; an arson attack in June 2009 on Greenwich Islamic Centre, and the near-blinding of a woman wearing a hijab in Rochdale by an attacker who said they supported and voted for the BNP.

One Society Many Cultures—defending multiculturalism

The aim in Britain must be to prevent what has happened in other European countries from happening here, both in terms of significant electoral breakthroughs by the far-right and fascist organisations and the advance of Islamophobia.

The One Society Many Cultures campaign brings Muslim communities together with other faiths, trade unions, academics and others. It believes that a movement opposing Islamophobia must ensure that the Muslim communities are at the centre of it—those who are most under attack must have the clearest voices in how to resist these attacks—but supported by other faith groups, the labour movement, politicians from all parties, civil libertarians and other activists and all those of goodwill who defend the values of our multicultural and diverse society.

In addition to campaigning against Islamophobia, defending the freedom of religion and cultural expression, the campaign will assert the benefits of a society where everyone is free to express their faith and culture how they choose, socially, economically and politically.

In Europe ideologically undermining the concept of multiculturalism was the prism through which bans on religious dress, the construction of minarets and so on were implemented. This is why campaigning against David Cameron's speech attacking multiculturalism was crucial. To summarise, Cameron's logic is that multiculturalism is a problem because it has led to segregation and separation of communities, and this has led to the growth of Islamic extremism and terrorist attacks. However, he failed to propose an alternative to multiculturalism. There is no evidence that shows society is becoming more segregated, in fact academic studies by Danny Dorling,[9] Ludi Simpson[10] and Ceri Peach[11] indicate that society is becoming more integrated.

Britain has been multicultural for thousands of years. We are a nation built on waves of immigration. Multiculturalism has enriched society in ways we take for granted: the food we eat, the music we listen to and indeed our heritage. By celebrating multiculturalism we create a more cohesive and integrated society in which it would be difficult for both fascism and extremism in Muslim communities to flourish.

That is why we have launched the One Society Many Cultures campaign.[12]

By allowing all communities to express their faith and culture—from religious Muslims to punks—everyone is free to be what they want, and faith and culture are no obstacle to feeling "British".

Leicester—one of Britain's most multicultural cities—is testimony to this. Leicester City Council actively promotes multiculturalism and unity through its "One Leicester" campaign. Research by the Open Society Institute found that in Leicester 72 percent of Muslims born abroad said they felt British with 94 percent of those born in Britain saying the same.

Celebrating multiculturalism is part of the fight against extremism, not the cause.

Multicultural Britain—
that's just the way it is

◆◆

DANNY DORLING

Over the course of the last century and a half Britain has benefited from immigration from a wider range of countries than anywhere else with comparable records. This has been the most beneficial legacy of empire and is the one thing at which Britain now excels in Western Europe. Britain is one of the most diverse of European countries by ethnic, national, religious and cultural origin. The graph below shows just a small collection of the countries that now contribute to the diversity of UK origins.

The remainder of this chapter is largely based on work first undertaken for the Runnymede Trust in an attempt to answer the question of who the working class might be losing out to when multiculturalism is attached, but it is reprinted here in the light of the recent and vicious attacks on multicultural Britain by people who think that it is somehow British to attack Britain. A century ago it was those who were seen as Jewish extremists who were targeted by the right wing in Britain. Today it is Muslims.

In David Cameron's infamous Munich speech he said "Islam is a religion, observed peacefully and devoutly by over a billion people. Islamist extremism is a political ideology, supported by a minority. At the furthest end are those who back terrorism to promote their ultimate goal: an entire Islamist realm, governed by an interpretation of Sharia. Move along the spectrum, and you find people who may reject violence, but who accept various parts of the extremist world view including real hostility towards western democracy and liberal values".[1]

People born abroad living in Britain 1841-2006

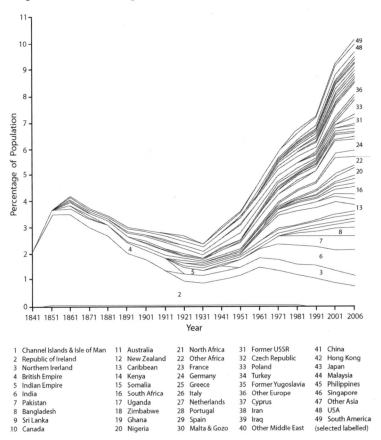

1	Channel Islands & Isle of Man	11	Australia	21	North Africa	31	Former USSR	41	China

Source: Bethan Thomas—see Dorling, D (2011) *So You Think You Know About Britain,* *London Constable,* for more details.

Read it again. The last sentence can be translated as: you may not advocate violence, but if you do not believe in David Cameron's world view then he and his friends may choose to label you as extremist, anti-democratic, or illiberal; and then he will lump you together in a "spectrum" which includes terrorists. Either you are with David Cameron, and fall within his definition of western democracy, liberal values and anti-extremism, or you too are part of a very violent problem. This is how you demonise people.

Once you start to demonise it's hard to stop. In his April 2011 follow-up speech David suggested next that "immigration and welfare reform are two sides of the same coin. Put simply, we will never control immigration properly unless we tackle welfare dependency. That's another powerful reason why this government is undertaking the biggest shake-up of the welfare system for generations…making sure that work will always pay…and ending the option of living a life on the dole when a life in work is possible".

So, according to David, people come to Britain because they are looking forward to a life on the dole. Immigrants make up large numbers of his imagined army of feckless scroungers (so-called welfare dependents). This kind of talking could also be found a century ago in Britain when the targets were supposedly feckless paupers and again Jews and the Irish. However, in recent years and across the globe, the tactics of spreading fear of "foreigners", "immigrants" and even refugees has been honed to an art as the following long extract from an academic paper makes clear:

> Politicians in the quest for votes have generated and manipulated public fears and then claimed to have allayed them. Margaret Thatcher, for example, argued in 1978 that British culture would be swamped by migrants—as if British culture were a fixed and definitive condition… News media have created or fuelled scares to improve ratings and attract advertising revenue. Apparently responding to alarm generated in the British press about an increase in the arrival of migrants and asylum seekers in 2001, Home Secretary David Blunkett adopted the same hateful representation (for example, asserting that there was a danger that schools and other public institutions would be "swamped" by immigrants) and introduced a series of measures to deter asylum seekers from reaching the UK. In that year the United Nations High Commissioner for Refugees, Ruud Lubbers, became concerned at the deliberate elite-driven securitization of asylum seeking by the media and by politicians of mainstream parties to win elections in Australia, Austria, Denmark, Italy and the UK… As investigators have revealed

in considerable detail, John Howard's Liberal Party Government in Australia manipulated the boat people issue to mobilize voters in order to steal the clothes of the far right One Nation Party and overtake Labour in the November 2001 election... The government dramatically inflated the issue as a threat to the Australian homeland and to sovereign control...[2]

One result of these political tactics is that those of us who know these fears to be misplaced are forced to reiterate again a series of home truths. In the remainder of this chapter I do that, but I am beginning to wonder whether our time might not be better spent working out exactly which member of the narcissist British Brothers League[3] in 1901 made speeches most similar to those which Mr Cameron is giving now, over a century later.

Concerns for the "white working class" are most frequently expressed in terms of how they might be losing out to groups of people recently arrived in Britain—immigrants—most of whom, incidently, happen to be white also. In the remaining sections of this chapter I take a few commonly made assertions and suggest an answer to them, and what might be done to improve policy for poorer people in general.

1. "Immigration means we don't get houses for those that deserve them." True?

Without immigration much current housing in Britain would no longer be standing. In particular many immigrants in recent decades came to towns and cities in the north of England which would have been greatly depopulated otherwise. Their coming and remaining has been one of the primary reasons why housing has not had to be demolished on a large scale outside of Scotland. In contrast, in Glasgow, a city which did not attract that many immigrants in recent years, a great deal of housing has had to be demolished. Fewer immigrants results in fewer homes. A majority of immigrants to Britain from abroad now settle in the south of England. Here there is the least social housing and so almost all housing is not allocated on the basis of who most deserves a home, but on who can afford a home (or homes). More and more housing has been bought to be rented privately, or as a second or third home by richer people. We have never had as much housing in Britain as we have now, but we have also never shared it out as badly as now.

Recent immigrants to Britain tend to be the worst housed, living in the most overcrowded accommodation and in some of the worst quality properties. Concerns are often expressed over who is housed first in social housing. Recent immigrants without children have almost no chance of being housed in such housing because of the rules of allocation, based upon need. We do not have enough social housing for everyone's needs in Britain. We do have enough housing in general for everyone's needs. What we need is a way of transferring more homes that people cannot afford to pay a mortgage on to social housing so that there is enough social housing for all who need it. This could be done if the current government programme that allows local authorities to buy a few repossessed homes at auction were extended so that people could sell their homes to the local council but remain living in them when they hit hard times. That "right to sell" would increase the stock of social housing. If it were coupled with policies to encourage people owning multiple empty homes to give up some of their spare houses, and to help single people in very large houses downsize, that would also help. Then we might get the housing we deserve.

2. "Immigration is a drain on the health services." True?

Health services in Britain only work because of immigration. In fact there are more nurses from Malawi working in Manchester alone than there are in Malawi. Immigrants and the next generation of children of immigrants make up a vastly disproportionate number of the staff of the National Health Service (NHS). Any sensible calculation of the net effect of immigration on health services could not conclude that there is any drain on resources. There is, however, an obvious drain on the health services of other countries from our reliance on so many staff from abroad. If more clinicians from Britain were to work at least part of their career abroad that effect would be somewhat offset, they would gain insight that they could not easily secure in Britain. They could have a significant impact worldwide.

There is a problem with accessing health services for some groups of recent immigrants, however. The National Health Service is not a national service. Often services are limited, such as dental care, and recent arrivals to an area can be put at a disadvantage because all NHS dentists are booked up. This affects all migrants, not just immigrants. More seriously, in 2004 proposals were made to further exclude overseas visitors from eligibility to use the NHS primary services. Only "ordinary residents" of the UK are entitled to free NHS treatment (someone living lawfully, voluntarily, for settled purposes). This regulation is particularly detrimental to anyone who has recently arrived in Britain who may find it hard to establish that they are ordinarily resident here. If someone is found not to be ordinarily resident then everything is charged for except immediate A&E care.

The Hippocratic Oath does not include a clause allowing this discrimination. The moral dilemma which doctors are faced with is also a moral dilemma confronting society as a whole. Do we really want to be the generation which dismantles the principle that a doctor's first concern is his or her patient, especially for such a spiteful cause? Working class people are often talked down to by middle and upper class doctors. Such doctors often resent the kind of work they find themselves doing. When they applied to go to medical school it did not cross their minds that they might, later, be asked to work with sick people all day. A better skilled medical workforce would provide a far better resource for working class people.

Medical staff who come from abroad are less likely to see people in Britain as beneath them. If our doctors routinely worked overseas following training then teenagers might think more carefully before applying to medical school. The experiences they would gain from abroad would also be useful. Younger doctors in Britain have usually not seen cases of measles and tuberculosis, but both diseases are becoming more common in Britain. When the influenza pandemic or any similar event does strike, all of us, including the white working class, would benefit from the knowledge and understanding of a more internationally experienced health workforce.

3. "My boy's the only white boy in his school—I can't leave him there can I?"

There are many ways in which children can be the only one in their school. Often this is hidden. For instance being the only child to be living with your grandparents, the only child who has a particular illness, or being the only child to have reached grade 7 on the violin. When other children find out that someone is unique they can be badly teased and bullied; but all children are unique in many ways and all can be teased and bullied. In every class one child will be tallest, shortest, fattest, thinnest, have the most spots, the least friends, go through puberty first, or last. Being the only white boy in a class is just one of the "only" things your boy may be. Hopefully, it may well be the least of any problems he has. And it may well be your problem, not his. However, if your child is being bullied because he is white, that is different from being bullied for having spots.

Racist bullying is not equal to other types of bullying; it can lead to race hate violence. Racist bullying is usually worse because it is more structural and systematic, and it is more likely to persist and then translate into other forms of discrimination later in life. Being bullied for being the only child playing the violin is unlikely to follow that child into the job market. No bullying should be tolerated but especially racist bullying. Your white child's skin colour will not disadvantage him in the job market, but no form of racist bullying can be tolerated because of where it leads a society. Would you want your son to adopt racist views because he was bullied? If the problem is teasing and bullying, then like any parent, you should expect the school to take it seriously and talk to all the children responsible—and their parents too.

If all children went to their nearest school there would be slightly fewer schools in which a single child was white, or of any other category. There would still, however, be a great number where there was only one child who was not white in a class. But if all children went to their nearest school it is likely that far fewer people would notice this anymore. That is because if there was one non-white child say in a village school, it would be because there was one non-white child in the village, not because that school had an admissions policy making it harder for other non-white children to gain entry (being "faith" based for instance, linked to a particular denomination).

4. "But how do we stop schools becoming more segregated?"

There is no evidence that schools in Britain are becoming more segregated by ethnicity but they are more segregated than are the neighbourhoods they draw from. It is very likely that they will become less segregated over time as the areas the schools are in have been becoming less segregated. The way in which schools are becoming more segregating is by whether the children in them come from poor, average, or rich homes. The great new range of schools that the current government has created has been compared to Britain introducing a new caste system, with differing schools, academies, beacon and "bog-standard" establishments catering for children thought of as being of differing inherent abilities. This is very bad news for all our children, rich and poor, black or white.

If children go to the nearest school: 1) they can walk rather than be driven; 2) the schools mix; 3) almost all children from the same street go to the same school so know each other; 4) fewer schools will appear to be very bad, nor will parents have to worry so much about trying to get into "good" schools; 5) there will be fewer schools where your son is the only white (or black, or brown, or whatever) boy in the school; 6) there will be no single sex schools.

Why in some cities are schools more segregated than the residential areas which surround them? The reason for this is mainly the last and new coalition government's "choice" agenda; in reality, low-income black and Asian parents find it harder to exercise choice and tend to downgrade their options. Most will send their children to the nearest secondary school due to size of family, convenience, lack of access to own transport and avoidance of high crime areas. Importantly this is not an issue of self-segregation, as most BME parents prefer their children to go to ethnically diverse schools. Rather, it's an issue of resources. If we reverted to the system of our parents' time, when almost all children went to their nearest school, you might think that schools would become more segregated by wealth as areas are so segregated by wealth and poverty. This is not necessarily true, however, as part of the attraction of some wealthy areas is that local schools are seen as especially good, tend to be over-subscribed, and those parents more able to argue their child's case to get their children in. Here "arguing" includes pretending to have religious beliefs for long enough to fool the selecting panels of the largest group of discriminatory schools in the country— the faith schools.

If all children went to their nearest schools then the few poor children living in richer neighbourhoods would be almost certain to go to their neighbourhood school and the school would appear slightly less "exclusive", house prices would become slightly less elevated and so on. Similarly, if all children in poor areas went to their local school, schools in poor areas would not appear as poor as they currently do. That is because currently there is massive commuting out to schools from poor areas. A policy of children only receiving free state education and going to their local school would probably reduce segregation in schools by income, wealth and race, but not by much because children are already so segregated geographically. To further reduce segregation between schools would require parents to have less incentive to segregate themselves by geography, would need them to live in less fear.

If schools were better resourced according to the needs of their pupils then it would make less sense for a parent to try to get their child into a "good" school by living in a "good" area. More would be spent on their education were they to go to a school where children needed more resources. In practical terms a primary school at the "bottom of the hill" in the poorer district might have two classroom teachers and two teaching assistants for a class of 30 children as compared to one at the "top of the hill" having half as many staff. The precise ratios should be set at the levels at which it no longer matters to a rational parent where on the hill they live. You can tell when it no longer matters as then more parents choose the "poorer" school. It is, in effect, a policy of "bussing" additional staff to schools with low demand. It would only be a policy that would be feasible when people in this country realise the value of educating their children as higher than many other ways we currently spend tax money (supporting American war efforts for instance).

5. "Multiculturalism or Britain—I have to choose sides, don't I?"

British society is a multicultural society so it is difficult to see what you would be choosing between if you were to try to choose. Every so often a politician or journalist suggests that it is time to make some choices. Some form of patriotism is needed. Often sport is involved or a perceived aspect of a thing they call "Britishness". These events are usually embarrassing. The temptation is to shy away and leave them to their ramblings. Occasionally, however, other people pick up on such suggestions and so it might help to choose to be on the side that knows a little bit about British and world history, cultures and multiculturalism, rather than on the side of ignorance. For example, often things that are thought of as being especially British, "tolerance" is an example, are not especially British. Often people in Britain are not especially good at things thought to be especially British, such as fairness.

What people in Britain are unusually good at, compared with almost all of the rest of the rich world, is multiculturalism. Most countries in Europe do not have people from such a range of places as in Britain. People from different ethnic groups are permitted to mix far less in a country like the United States of America as compared to Britain. In the US you will rarely see black and white couples together on television; there is a taboo against it. In contrast again, that often forgotten large population of the rich world, Japan, currently severely limits immigration. Japan is the fastest-ageing large population on the planet. A majority of adults in Japan are now living on their own in single person households, such is population aging there. People in Japan are going to find coping with the immigration to come there much harder than we do in Britain. We could perhaps help.

Multiculturalism is Britain. It is one of the things that is quite special about Britain and which makes Britain less like other countries. If Britain were a less socially divided country, if working class people were not so poor compared to middle class people, and if middle class people were not so poor as compared to upper class people, then there may not be such recognisable differences in Britain. Countries with much lower income inequalities, such as Iceland and Japan, have become far less concerned about the different cultures within those countries.

You hear very little talk of different Japanese or Icelandic ethnicities. This is not because these two sets of islands are home to
remarkably homogeneous ethnic groups, but because income and
wealth inequalities are so much lower there. We often mistake the
wealth divisions of Britain for multicultural differences. Britain is a
country divided by wealth, but brought together by the many cultures that have found their way here over the centuries. Incidentally,
attitudes to immigrants in both Iceland and Japan are hardly a model
of tolerance; people can appear overtly racist and are far less careful
about their language than in Britain. Those few migrants that there
are, from Eastern Europe and mainly Korea respectively, are greatly
exploited. In both countries income inequalities are growing, yet in
both, because of their more equitable social histories, life expect-
ancy is much longer than in that third set of islands, Britain. In the
case of Iceland, as in much of the rest of Scandinavia, the rarity of
resources made greater equality more necessary and a redistributive
welfare state attempts to maintain that (although wealth inequalities
are growing). In Japan it was the confiscation of land from the aris-
tocracy and its redistribution by the American occupying forces that
had the same equalising outcome (and it is very different mechanisms
that maintain it). In Japan, wealth inequalities are currently falling
but income inequality is rising. Had the histories of both countries
been different, had Iceland been the centre of a world empire with
American colonies, had Japan entered the Second World War on the
side of America, race and ethnicity would mean very different things
in both places.

6. "What's worse than getting Polish workers in your town?"

Not getting Polish workers in your town! Have you tried getting someone to fix a leaking tap recently? More seriously, hardly any Polish
immigrants are plumbers, but the Polish workers who have come to
Britain are generally highly skilled and almost all go to where they are
needed. If there are none where you live it is most probably because
people where you live are not making enough money to employ them;
businesses where you live are not expanding enough to need them; or

where you live is really not that desirable a place to come to.

Often Polish workers are vastly over-skilled for the work they are doing in Britain. Recent Polish immigration is not qualitatively different from other recent streams of immigration from abroad. When I first wrote this I said "Luckily for people in much of Britain in 2008 we are still seen as a desirable destination for significant numbers of migrants from abroad". And that "The numbers who come here roughly match the numbers of people born in Britain who travel to work and live overseas". Sadly that is no longer true—as the economic crash now means that far fewer people could find work if they came here so they have started not to come and many people are leaving Britain to find jobs and a future.

It is only because people come here that we have the freedom to travel and work abroad without there being a great detrimental effect on the economy in Britain. Every so often a few more people come into Britain than leave. 2008 was just one of those times. It is very fortunate for us that they do so, because since the early 1970s women in Britain have been having fewer than two babies on average. Sadly many of the Polish workers are likely to move on before they have children. Britain has 1 percent of the world's population but only 0.5 percent of the world's children.

As the British economy entered recession we saw that fewer people from Poland and other places chose to come here. Countries like Germany opened up their borders to free movement of labour with Poland. People from Britain in a recession tend to go to work in places like Germany, to become immigrants abroad. This is especially true for working class men; usually their wives and children are left at home in Britain while they work abroad. You will be able to tell when the bad times are coming when the migrants from abroad stop coming, and some start leaving. Whether you will be able to carry on living where you live, or whether you will have to move to look for work elsewhere, or even go abroad, will depend on the extent to which your government decides to look after people in Britain. During the last major long-lasting recession, in the early 1980s, the government chose not to do this. Far more people left Britain than came in during those years. Many never returned.

7. "Living separately is a problem, isn't it?"

We all "live separately" and we all have links outside where we live, even if just outside the street. More and more of us live separately despite being in long term relationships, and families in Britain now tend to be far more spread out and separated between places than they have ever been. Living less crowded lives is part of what we secure from being more affluent, but that is not what those who use this phrase are really talking about when they say there is a problem. What they are concerned about is a perception that people of Muslim faith tend not to mix, shop, play, go to school, or work with other people as much as they might if such things were random. However, life is not random. People don't mix from different areas in all sorts of ways.

People don't tend to mix from Hinksey and Barton on opposite sides of Oxford, or Dore and Brightside on opposite sides of Sheffield. If we meet different kinds of people it tends to be in the centre of town. Should we be worried about this? Not really, unless someone sets us against each other or says we should move when we don't want to. In fact, we live separately in all sorts of ways—according to our income, how ill we are, what kinds of jobs we have—and that separation is getting worse at the same time as separation according to our race or colour is getting less (these things are measured by segregation indices).

People who have looked at it find that the level of separation between Muslims and others is not at all large in regions such as Yorkshire and Humberside. When you think of "Muslim" areas in the region you will usually think of places that actually are very diverse. Of the 35 districts in Britain that had one ward at the last census with fewer than 50 percent white residents, only one of them was in Yorkshire and Humberside. That one district is Bradford, and even there it's a minority white ward—called "University" ward—which had 25 percent white residents, hardly a separation. During the year before the census, more white residents came to that ward from other parts of the UK than left it and more black and Asian residents left the ward than came to it: so it is becoming more mixed from migration, not a separate ghetto.

Mixing takes place at the most intimate level too, in spite of all that talk about what people would let their daughter, and occasionally son, do! According to the census, a greater proportion of Muslims marry non-Muslims than white Christians marry outside "their" group. That's simply because most white Christians live in areas where there is no-one else to meet, and it shows how much easier it is for white folk to segregate than it is for other people to keep to themselves. People in mixed relationships are often ostracised. It was far worse in the 1970s and early 1980s when mixed couples often had to give up their children to adoption due to pressure from families and friends. Those days have gone for most, but not for all.

8. "Why don't they speak English? They are holding themselves back."

The government in England wants everyone to speak English fluently, but has cut funding for English classes. It says we should speak more foreign languages, but criticises those who do! The administration in Wales wants more people to speak, read and write Welsh, but the government in England often forget this. There are very few people who cannot speak English at all in England. There are very many people in England who can only speak English. Most people in the world can speak more than one language, but not so in England. We are holding ourselves back by not expanding our vocabulary.

Almost all people in England welcome help to speak and read or write better. But just like anyone they do not relish being insulted or put down in their attempts to improve. By far the largest group of people who need help with their English speak, read a little, and write even less only English. Millions of adults in Britain are functionally illiterate. Everyone who finds English or Welsh difficult and who wants to learn should be helped to do better. Equally we need to learn other languages to better understand the rest of the world and each other. Otherwise we really are holding ourselves back.

Recently there has been official advice against providing translation services, documents in other languages, even providing translators when mothers are giving birth or people are at criminal trials. It should only take you a few second to imagine how terrifying it would be for you to be giving birth and for no-one around you to understand you, or to be trying to defend yourself in a court of law in your second or third language. The British are among the least literate people on the planet, partly because they can mostly get by just in English. But we expect things to be in English when we go abroad, or buy goods on the internet. We don't call ourselves immigrants when abroad, but "expats". We need to learn more about English and no longer behave as if we run a global empire.

9. "Does white flight really have wings?"

No. People move when they can get better housing and a better environment, when they can no longer afford the house they are living in, or when they grow up and leave home. They tend to move short distances unless they move to get an education or to a job a long way away. Those who have a bit more money can afford to move where they want to go, and move a bit further. The research on migration shows that the things that are associated with moving are the same for all ethnic groups in Britain.

In Yorkshire and Humberside there are only five districts with a concentration of black and Asian residents as high as 20 percent in one of their wards. If there was white flight you might expect there to be white people leaving those wards. But the census shows that white people did not leave Batley East in Kirklees, or University area in Bradford, or Burngreave in Sheffield, for other parts of the UK: more white people went to those wards than left them. And in the other two districts, where there was movement of white residents out of the 'black and Asian concentrations', there is also movement of black and Asian residents out of the same areas. So for example in the year before the census, both white and other residents left Harehills in Leeds, and St Johns in Calderdale, the areas in each district that had the lowest white population. But we can see that some areas are becoming "more Asian" and "less white". Whatever people say about why they move, the figures show that this isn't because White people are moving out more than Asians. The inner areas are getting "more Asian" for two other reasons. First it is because there are few older Asians yet—those who immigrated mostly did so only 30 or 40 years ago—so there will be relatively few Asians dying until the next couple of decades. Second, it is because there is still some immigration of wives and husbands.

The circulation of immigrants and their families first to inner city areas where there is cheap housing, and then out to better housing when they can afford to do so, is the same as the Irish and Jewish immigration last century. Over time people get used to each other—unless there is continued racism or discrimination that keeps some people in the worst housing. Where social inequalities between people are allowed to be high and rise, racism follows.

10. Conclusion—"How would you like it if you lived here?"

I wouldn't. I don't live in a poor neighbourhood, but I do live in an increasingly ethnically mixed neighbourhood. Thinking that your neighbours are your problem is a distraction from looking out at who really has what you don't have. Ask yourself this:

Why are there people who can live in a flat in the middle of your city during the week, but are living somewhere else at the weekend? Why are there people who only come to their "homes" a few times a year? Where else are they living? Why is there no longer any social housing in the countryside, or almost none? If you are poor there are unlikely to be many second homes near where you live, but where you live will be more crowded than if people today were spread between flats and houses as they were a couple of decades ago. In London the very rich are converting previously subdivided houses back into their original grand sizes, reducing the stock of housing for everyone else. Many of the richest million people on the planet own a house or flat in London as well as many homes elsewhere. Although there may be a servant household living in their London home, these second, third and fourth home owners have removed up to one million homes from being available in the capital alone.

There is enough housing in Britain for everyone to be housed. There are at least twice as many bedrooms in homes in Britain as there are people to sleep in those bedrooms. The same can be said of school books, of medicines, of jobs, of money. Britain is an extremely rich country, but it is one of those rich countries of the world where people have found it harder to learn how to share than elsewhere. Because we find it harder to share, we tend to be mistrustful. That mistrust results in fear, fear in the rich of the poor, fear in the poor of immigrants, fear in immigrants of prejudice. We need somewhere to go in place of fear. We live mostly in fear of monsters we have created in our dreams, but those monsters then become very real. It is our ignorance and stupidity, and our ability to be taken for a ride by those who already have most, which we should be most frightened of.

◆ The original version of this paper was published by the Runnymede Trust under the title "From Housing to Health—To Whom are the White Working Class Losing Out? Frequently Asked Questions" in *Runnymede Perspectives: Who Cares About the White Working Class*, edited by Kjartan Páll Sveinsson, Runnymede Trust, January 2009. An electronic version can be read or downloaded from the Runnymede website www.runnymedetrust.org

◆ We are grateful to the Runnymede Trust for their kind permission to reproduce this updated version.

MULTICULTURALISM BY ZITA HOLBOURNE[1]

I embrace my Multiculturalism
As I do my Afrocentrism
As I do my Feminism
And even my *Englishism*

I have African and European roots but I'm a Londoner
I'm both Caribbean and an Eastender
My Sunday dinners include both roast potatoes and *rice n peas*
I can slip between 'BBC English', 'Cockney' and 'Patois' *with ease*
I was raised in the church but respect all religion
Some of my friends are atheist but doesn't cause division
I relax with Jazz, dance to Hip Hop
Chill with Lovers, but I love BeBop!

You can't define me with a single entity
That's because I have a multiple identity
I'm not just *multicultural*
I'm also multiracial

I'm proud of my history and my roots
I dress, speak and communicate as it suits
You can't define me with just *one* word
To limit my multiculture would *be* absurd!

The complexities of my multiple identities
Manifest in my eccentricities
They're wrapped up in my DNA, my blood, invasion, freedom
In Empire, enslavement, in race, belief, religion
In class and gender, language and dialect
Skills and talent, knowledge and intellect
Add to this the food I eat, the music I adore
The traditions I embrace and the passions I live for

If *I* am *multicultured* as *I* alone stand
I'm afraid *Mr Prime Minister*, I don't **understand**
How you expect a whole population *collectively*
To be single cultured and have just **one** *identity*
And how you can believe multiculturalism's dead
When I'm a living legacy of it's success

It's ***deep rooted***, sometimes understated
Always there but never overrated
It's in the way we ***sing*** and the way we talk
The way we dance and the way we walk

Multiculturalism cannot fail to succeed
It's not in the gift of a politician to proceed
With it's termination
IT'S NOT YOUR CREATION!
It's in our blood and in our bones
You can't create multicultural free zones

It's on our airwaves and in our streets
In our attire and rhythm and beats
It's in street food and haute cuisine
It's even in her Majesty the Queen
It's in the theatre and in literature
In places of worship and holy scripture

It's **CELEBRATION!**
It's **JUBILATION!**
It's pomp and glory
And it's **OUR STORY!**

You *can't erase what makes us who we are!*
It's not something you can permit or bar!
And you can't take away what brings us *together*
RECOGNISE *Mr Prime Minister*
MULTICULTURALISM's **here forever!**

SECTION TWO

HORRIBLE HISTORIES
MYTHS OF TOLERANCE AND NATIONHOOD

A place of refuge?
Scapegoating "the other"—
the treatment of Jewish refugees

◆◆

EDIE FRIEDMAN

Their unclean habits, their wretched clothing and miserable food enable them to perpetuate existence upon a pittance...these immigrants
have flooded the labour market with cheap labour to such an extent to
reduce thousands of native workers to the verge of destitution... Surely
our own people have the first claim upon us.[1]

Looking back at the popular press's descriptions of Jewish refugees in
the 1880s, it is clear that little has changed in the intervening century
in terms of language and tone.[2] In fact the history of Jewish migration
to Britain offers numerous parallels with the refugee experience today,
as well as echoing some of the vagaries of current government policies,
social provision, public opinion and media coverage.

The years from 1880-1914 were a period of continuous persecution, harassment and economic deprivation for Jews in Eastern
Europe. During this period over three million Jews left Russia,
Poland and Romania to escape pogroms,[3] poverty and conscrip-
tion into the Russian army, the latter sometimes lasting as long as 20
years. Britain's Jewish community grew from 60,000 in 1880 to about
300,000 in 1914.

The arrival of such large numbers of refugees was met with a less
than rapturous welcome by the government, the trade unions, certain newspapers and indeed sections of the Jewish community itself.
Moreover, their arrival was the catalyst for the formation of several
antisemitic groups including the British Brothers League in 1900, in
some ways a forerunner of the British Union of Fascists. To begin with,

the Trades Union Congress fomented this anti-immigration debate, passing a number of resolutions between 1892 and 1895 calling for strict anti-alien legislation.[4] Inevitably, a number of politicians were happy to jump on this bandwagon. The Conservative Party made alien restriction a central plank of its party platform after the 1900 general election.[5]

Until the end of the 19th century, refugees from European political regimes were largely welcomed by successive governments and were not subject to immigration restraints. It was not until the large-scale immigration of Jews from Russia and Eastern Europe that the 1905 Aliens Act was passed, restricting the entry of "undesirable and destitute immigrants" who were considered to be a charge on public funds or posed a risk to public health.[6]

This Act included a provision to deport immigrants and in its first four years 1,378 Jews were deported, many of whom had lived with their families in the UK for years. Some of these deportations were done with the approval of the Jewish community. In 1888 the then main Jewish communal organisation in Britain, The Board of Guardians, prided itself on having arranged and funded repatriation of thousands of Jewish families.[7] Far more numerous were those refugees who were given financial and housing assistance by institutions within the Jewish community created precisely to help the new arrivals. But the generosity shown by some in the Jewish community was somewhat tempered by pressures from more settled Jews for the "newcomers" to give up some of their "foreign ways". In 1881 the main British Jewish newspaper, *The Jewish Chronicle*, stated:

> If they intend to remain in England, if they wish to become members of our community, we have a right to demand that they will show signs of an earnest wish for a complete amalgamation with the aims and the feelings of their host.[8]

The 1905 Aliens Act was followed by two subsequent acts of parliament, the Aliens Restrictions Acts of 1914 and 1919, which further limited the entry of aliens and restricted the movement of those already here, "adding a heavy dose of post-war xenophobia and

Horrible histories: Myths of tolerance and nationhood

anti-Bolshevism to what were already extreme measures".[9]

The anti-alienism expressed during this period by a number of politicians, trade unions, certain sections of the press (and some quarters of the Jewish community itself) was to resurface after the next major wave of Jewish refugees in 1933 and again during subsequent waves of other refugees to Britain in the late 20th and early 21st centuries.

The Jewish refugees who came in 1933 did so as a direct result of Hitler's accession to power. Initially, the United Kingdom's policy was directed at not interfering in Germany's so-called internal affairs. This view was reinforced by the belief that the arrival of Jewish refugees would be at variance with Britain's economic interests. There was, nevertheless, concerted pressure from a number of Jewish organisations as well as MPs and some church groups to admit more Jewish refugees. In 1938 the annexation of Austria (Anschluss), and the German pogroms of 9-10 November (Kristallnacht—literally "The Night of Broken Glass"—antisemitic riots in which Jews were physically attacked and many synagogues destroyed) put increased pressure on the government to relax restrictions on refugees. Between Kristallnacht and the start of the war, 40,000 Jewish refugees were granted temporary residency in Britain.[10]

The fact that Britain took in these Jewish refugees has an iconic importance for our self-definition today as a generous and welcoming nation to the downtrodden of the world. As shown by the anniversaries of the end of the Second World War, the emphasis has been on Britain's heroic role, not only in defeating the Nazis but also in providing a haven for Jewish refugees. Some people even believe that Britain went to war in order to save the Jews, though there is no evidence to support this view. The reality was rather different: there was considerable antagonism towards the refugees from all sections of society, and especially from some trade unions and certain sections of the press. An editorial in the *Sunday Express* in 1938 stated:

> [But] just now there is a big influx of foreign Jews into Britain. They are over-running the country. They are trying to enter the medical profession in great numbers. They wish to practise as dentists. Worst of all, many of them are holding themselves out to the public as

psychoanalysts. There is no intolerance in Britain today. And by keeping a close watch on the causes that feed the intolerance of the Jews in other European countries, we shall be able to continue to treat well those Jews who have made their homes among us.[11]

In some sections of society antisemitism was quite overt. The actress Joyce Grenfell remarked, "There is something a bit uncosy about a non-Aryan refugee in one's kitchen".[12]

Resistance also came from trade and professional bodies. Jewish refugee doctors trying to come to Britain before the war, for instance, had a difficult time. With the exception of the Socialist Medical Association, prominent medical organisations such as the British Medical Association and the Medical Practitioners Union lobbied to ensure that these refugee doctors would not be allowed into Britain before the war as they would "dilute our industry". A scheme to bring in 500 Austrian doctors before the war was rejected. Historian Tony Kushner quotes the infamous comment made by Lord Dawson, president of the Royal College of Physicians in 1933: "The number of refugee doctors who could usefully be absorbed, or teach us anything, could be counted on the fingers of one hand".[13]

Negative attitudes towards Jewish refugees were also found in the Foreign Office, in contrast to more humanitarian concerns expressed by the Home Office:

> Senior Home Office officials were overwhelmingly sympathetic towards Jews. In this respect they compare favourably with their counterparts in the Foreign Office. Certainly, hostility towards Jews contributed to the lassitude with which Foreign Office officials generally responded to proposals for humanitarian aid to Jews and to the vigour with which they argued against giving such aid.[14]

General anti-Jewish prejudice was instrumental in formulating government policy:

> What we can say is that British stereotypes of Jews were significant in marking them out as members of a group that was difficult, even

dangerous, to help. Such prejudices helped to cast the image of the Jewish refugee in a problematic mould and thus to strengthen support for policies of restriction.[15]

At the same time, many non-Jews were sympathetic to the refugees, as were some religious organisations such as the Quakers. The Attenboroughs (parents of film director Richard, now Lord Attenborough, and Sir David Attenborough, the natural historian and broadcaster) adopted two Jewish children who came on the Kindertransport (a government-sponsored programme in 1938-39 to admit Jewish children from Germany and the German-occupied territories, though not their parents).

By the start of the war, about 80,000 Jewish refugees had come to Britain, including 10,000 unaccompanied children on the Kindertransport.[16] (The United States refused to instigate a similar scheme on the grounds that it was against the will of God to separate children from their parents.) In addition, 20,000 women were allowed to enter the country as domestic servants. [17]

Asylum in the United Kingdom was dependent on guarantees that the Jewish community would provide for all of the refugees' needs. Unsurprisingly, such a financial undertaking could not be sustained and the government was eventually forced into providing some assistance. While there was a huge amount of work done by Jewish individuals and organisations to help the refugees, the Jewish establishment itself was at times reluctant to demand that greater numbers should be allowed into Britain,[18] "since political action qua Jews was precisely what they'd relinquished in return for civil rights and might, they feared, be taken both as a criticism of the British government and in gratitude, thereby generating domestic antisemitism".[19]

Nevertheless, many individuals and organisations within the Jewish community rallied to lobby the government to allow in more refugees and then worked assiduously to assist in their integration after their arrival.

As the situation for European Jewry deteriorated, the British government's behaviour did not alter fundamentally: "The problem of what to do with the Jews took precedence over saving them".[20]

Thus Britain's overall response to the plight of Jews was character-ised by "caution and pragmatism subordinating humanitarianism to Britain's self-interest".[21] It was also felt that their very presence would encourage even more antisemitism.[22] This belies the national myth that Britain went to war to save the Jews.

After the war, Britain's policy towards Jewish refugees became more restrictive.[23] Over 600,000 work permits were given out to displaced persons from Europe, of which only a few thousand went to Jews. In a post-war Britain experiencing an acute labour shortage, Jews did not fit into the "economic requirements" it demanded: they were neither considered good workers nor were they thought likely to assimilate into the British way of life. This view was similar to the official think-ing before the war:

> The Jews were not a pressing problem so long as they remained in the Nazis' clutches. Jews would cause serious international embarrass-ment only if they escaped and became refugees... Jewish refugees were expected to arouse hostility and states were reluctant to accept them as immigrants.[24]

Children were the main beneficiaries of the government's post-war policy towards Jewish refugees, though compared to the need, its response was inadequate. The Home Office devised a policy to allow 1,000 Jewish orphans into the country on a temporary basis, though only 732 met their strict criteria. The policy towards adults was less generous. Under the Distressed Relatives Scheme, a paltry 1,200 Jews were allowed into the country. The US, which had a more stringent approach to accepting Jewish refugees both before and during the war, made some amends after the war by allowing in 100,000 refugees. In assessing Britain's record towards Jewish refugees, "the conclusion can-not be avoided. Escape to Britain was an experience for a lucky few. Exclusion was the fate of the majority".[25] This is in spite of an opinion poll conducted in 1943 which showed that 78 percent of the respond-ents were in favour of admitting endangered Jews.[26]

Even after the war, however, anti-Jewish feelings still surfaced, as illustrated by a little-known episode in Hampstead, in north west

London, where many German Jewish refugees had settled. Around 3,000 residents signed a petition in October 1945 demanding that "aliens of Hampstead" should be repatriated in order to free up housing for returning servicemen and women:

> ...despite the emerging details regarding the depths of Nazi racial barbarity, the plight of Jewish refugees in Britain was not followed by a wave of compassion and reparation. Against a backdrop of generalised sentiment in favour of repatriation, the Jewish refugee was often viewed not as a deserving recipient of sympathy, but as a parasitic interloper depriving Hampstead's indigenous citizens of scarce resources.[27]

The petition mirrored generalised anti-alien sentiment within Britain. *The Times* newspaper campaigned for the repatriation of "aliens" as a necessary prerequisite to reconstruct Europe. The term referred not only to Jews but also to Czechs, Poles and even the Free French. Thus refugees were charged with a two-pronged responsibility. The first was to stop using "our" resources as there were others whose claims was more deserving. The second was to "go back to where they came from" in order to aid in the reconstruction of their former country. Both arguments resonate with contemporary anti-asylum rhetoric: that government resources should be prioritised for British citizens and that asylum seekers should be repatriated for the sake of their home countries' development.

This antipathy towards Jewish refugees was a forewarning of "the even greater hostility which was to be faced by future generations of immigrants and asylum seekers".[28]

Press and politicians have created new "facts"—refugees are a problem, essentially parasitic on our society rather than contributing to it. They repeat the mantra that restricting the entry of refugees is a necessary prerequisite for the achievement of "good race relations".[29] Another common "fact" or myth is that refugees' claims are without substance. With press and politicians repeatedly reinforcing this notion, a false dichotomy of the so-called "genuine" and "bogus" refugee has entered the language. This distinction is used to discredit the legitimacy of a person's right to asylum: "the genuine refugee of popular mentality hardly exists in the here and now, but is firmly, and of course safely, located in the past where numbers are no longer a problem and action irrelevant".[30] And:

> It is thus ironic that the Jews from Eastern Europe at the turn of the 20th century and those escaping from the Third Reich in the 1930s have now become part of the elite club of historically designated "genuine refugees"—the latest members being the Ugandan Asians—whom "we" were right to help in the past. No politician or commentator, aside from those in neo-fascist organisations, would dare now to say that either the Huguenots or the Jews were anything but deserving of asylum.[31]

In 2002, the *Daily Express* claimed, "Most immigrants are not genuine asylum seekers. They are young single men who have deserted their families for money".[32]

This climate of disbelief recalls the response made by an official of the Foreign Office, Arminius Dew, in September 1944 to those he thought to be exaggerating the horrors of Nazi persecution: "In my opinion a disproportionate amount of the time of the office is wasted with these wailing Jews." And again: "What is distressing is the apparent readiness of the new Colonial Secretary to take this Jewish Agency 'sob stuff' at its face value".[33]

In order to counter the arguments and allegations made against refugees, refugee organisations have made efforts to highlight the contribution refugees make to our society. This was and still is a two-edged sword. On the one hand, it is appropriate to draw people's attention to the enormous contribution refugees have made in the past. On the other, an impression can be created that gaining asylum in this country should depend on whether or not asylum seekers/refugees have anything they can offer us. Are those with less significant skills not worthy of the same protection?

Playing the "numbers game"—playing down the number of asylum seekers and refugees who enter the United Kingdom—can have a further detrimental effect on the refugee community. Those supporting the refugees against the Hampstead petitioners argued that the numbers cited in the anti-alien petition were grossly exaggerated, but:

> whilst it was necessary to refute the false information given by the petitioners, this drive to play down the numbers of refugees, and by implication the influence they wield both within the district and nationally, had the unfortunate consequences of adding to the dehumanisation of the refugees' plight, which was lost in the cold set of easily quantifiable statistics.[34]

In addition to being labelled as undesirable by host communities and the government, refugees have also borne some antagonism from their own people who, although already established here, still live under a cloud of insecurity. It is borne of a fear that increased immigration, particularly of the poor and "culturally different", will exacerbate racism against the established minority communities. Throughout the century the Jewish establishment thought it imperative that Jewish refugees should acculturate as quickly as possible.[35]

These ambivalent attitudes were more recently echoed in a 1998 survey conducted by the Institute of Public Policy Research, which found that 48 percent of Asians interviewed believed there was too much Asian immigration into Britain.

One of the inevitable consequences of this ambivalence is pressure to give up certain aspects of one's culture in order to blend in with the dominant social group. Such anxieties are common to many refugees and immigrants, irrespective of where they come from or where they are going. Such a sentiment is vividly depicted by the journalist Yasmin Alibhai-Brown, herself a refugee from Idi Amin's Uganda, as she reflects on growing up in that country in the 1960s:

> I dressed in mock Victorian clothes and did not walk too close to relatives with "bad" accents. Others changed their names. Balwinders became Babs. We taught ourselves to forget how to eat rice with our hands and grappled foolishly with chicken legs as they flew off our forks. How Peter Sellers laughed. Thus we became adept at chiselling off any bits that might cause offence, trigger off painful rejections. But

they came anyway. To add insult, the more we tried to belong the less we were respected.[36]

The black peer, Ros Howells, makes a similar point about growing up in the Caribbean:

England was certainly the only place to come… It's like going to finishing school really… We didn't see England as a separate entity. For example, in my own convent school we spent a lot of time knitting little bits of wool for people during the war, you know the poor… We didn't see there was a difference between Grenada and England. "There will always be an England and England shall be free" used to be one of our school songs… Empire Day was big in Grenada.[37]

Not all similarities between refugee experiences past and present are negative. Both in the early 1900s and today many refugees have shown striking resilience in their fight against anti-immigrant/asylum legislation as well as in their wide range of cultural expression. The East End of London was home to a diverse artistic community, from the Yiddish theatre to avant-garde painters (Mark Gertler, David Bomberg), poets (Isaac Rosenberg) and playwrights (Bernard Kops, Harold Pinter, Arnold Wesker). Today, refugees from over 100 countries who now call Britain their home have organised hundreds of groups to cater for the needs of their respective communities and campaign for fairer asylum legislation. Those who are allowed to work are found in a wide array of skilled and unskilled jobs as well as teaching, law and medicine. Cultural expression is extensive and varied, ranging from the Iranian comedienne Shappi Khorsandi to the writer and Nobel Prize Winner, Wole Soyinka.

One area of improvement for refugees today is in the attention paid to their psychological needs. It provides a stark contrast with previous generations of refugees, most notably Holocaust survivors, who were discouraged from talking about their horrific experiences. Although recently more have been telling their stories, it wasn't until the 50th anniversary of the liberation of Auschwitz in 1995 that many Jewish survivors here felt they had "permission" to speak publicly about what had happened. A therapy centre for Holocaust survivors and their families was not established until 1990. In contrast, refugees today are encouraged to talk about their experiences as soon as they feel able. Post-traumatic stress disorder is now a well-recognised phenomenon and treatment centres such as the Medical Foundation for the Care of Victims of Torture have been set up, although these facilities tend to be under-resourced.[38]

Another area of improvement for contemporary refugees is the situation of refugee doctors. The antipathy shown by the medical establishment to Jewish refugee doctors in the 1930s has been replaced by a desire to ensure that their skills will not be lost. A great deal of work has gone into programmes to help today's refugee doctors to re-qualify, much of it spearheaded by the British Medical Association with financial support from the government.

Ironically, while children's rights are high on the political agenda, this is not matched by the treatment unaccompanied refugee children receive. Their predicament represents a failure to deal either compassionately or effectively with the situation.

Britain's image of itself, today as well as at the end of the 19th century, has been that of a country with a proud tradition of accepting those seeking sanctuary. It forms part of our national identity. But neither in the experience of Jewish refugees in the late 19th and early 20th century nor in the experience of those from Nazi-occupied Europe does this national myth entirely stand up. Rather, we are left with a picture of an ambivalent government that on the one hand proclaims its humanitarian commitments and on the other bows to populist opinion, reinforced by the inflammatory rhetoric of certain sections of the press and trade unions:

> The reality is that, since 1905, the most "generous" moments of British refugee policy have been the result of guilt, economic self-interest and international power politics, rather than of notions of "natural justice" per se.[39]

It is assumed by some that Britain has "done its bit" and can leave it to other countries to take in refugees; and that this country's compassion as well as its ability to cope with more refugees has been exhausted. However, in understanding the past and planning for the future a balanced view of British history is vital. It is also a necessary prerequisite for building a diverse and inclusive society. Unrealistic perceptions of our historical altruism cannot absolve us from our responsibilities towards refugees and asylum seekers today.

◆ This article first appeared as a chapter entitled "A Place Of Refuge? Case Study: Jewish Refugees As A Paradigm For The Refugee Experience" in the book *Reluctant Refuge: The Story of Asylum in Britain* by Edie Friedman and Reva Klein, published by the British Library in 2008. © Edie Friedman. The editor would like to thank the author for permission to reprint it.

Culture:
It's all in the mix!

❖❖

MICHAEL ROSEN

*W*ith David Cameron's words on multiculturalism reverberating round the gutters, now's a good time to take a second look at the word "culture". The two main overlapping ways the word is used in everyday conversation are: a) to cover artistic products we consume—plays, films, books, paintings and the like; b) to talk of the way we do things in our everyday lives—our "kinship" relations, what we eat and how we prepare it, what kind of dwellings, rituals, music, gestures we make and, significantly, what language(s), dialect(s) and accent(s) we speak with.

Underlying many discussions about the second use is the notion that there is a "host" culture which is distinct, unified, ancient, virtuous and desirable and there are "other" cultures which at best are "interesting" or "lively" but should be made to "integrate" or become "assimilated". As Marxists we might re-shape that and talk of a "dominant" or "hege-monic" culture and talk of "non-dominant" or "sub-cultures". Either way, this has its problems, because it presents cultures as if they are dis-crete chunks. From the right, there has been an effort to claim some kind of pure English or British "way of life" or "set of values" which is "indigenous". Meanwhile, on our side, we quite rightly celebrate mul-ticultural "diversity" and "minority cultures", claiming this as a form of cultural resistance. I think we have to go further than that and celebrate interculturalism—which is ultimately part of internationalism.

Human beings migrate. It is one of the conditions of humanity across time. Many times it has been in order to colonise and domi-nate other peoples—military and colonial migration, or transportation migrations where peoples have been taken forcibly across distances. Many times migration has been resistant, to escape persecution, overcrowding and poverty. Other times it has been in a more equitable form of exchange, where peoples have made contact with each other in order to trade goods and/or exchange ideas and art. In all these cases, the consequence is that cultures mix. With colonial migration there has been the spread of the English language, but wherever English has settled it has been re-shaped by the peoples of those places. Transportation has produced the explosion of diverse cultural forms as a consequence of Africans being enslaved across North and South America and the Caribbean and mixing with natives and Europeans. Resistant migration has resulted in such mixtures as "the post-colonial novel" or "Gipsy jazz", while trade migrations have given us Latin phrases like "et cetera" and, say, modernist architecture.

This inter-cultural mixing reaches into what is supposedly both "host" and somehow immune to this hybridisation. Even as the ruling class uses Britishness or Englishness in order to extend its domination into our minds, it is itself a mish-mash. The early development of "British" parliamentary democracy owes a good deal to the resistant cultures of dissenting Christians but this was never purely British. Puritanism was a fusion of European ideas—German, Swiss, Dutch, French, Scots and English. Much of the "English" landscape was shaped by migrants from continental Europe clearing forests or much later, draining land. Great "English" literature like Chaucer is in fact a mix of French, Italian and, in the "frame" device of the Canterbury Tales, Arab influence. Shakespeare's plays are written in Latinate blank verse with plot-lines borrowed from Denmark, Ancient Greece and Rome, Italy and beyond. Classical music is a trans-European phenomenon and one of the supposedly most "English" composers—Handel—was German. The "English" Beatles began and ended with the strains of the blues, Tamla Motown and rock which themselves were and are cultural hybrids. "British" education is made up of a mix of Greek, Roman, German, Swiss, French ideas as well as local ones. The Church of England is based on layers of Middle Eastern religions interfused with structures derived out of the religion's Italian establishment. And of course, even the idea of "nation" is international!

Horrible histories: Myths of tolerance and nationhood

What we do is endlessly assimilate to each other. It's asymmetrical—certain ideas "dominate", but not as those who dominate, describe it. The domination is achieved by inventing the myth of a pure centre while making the impossible demand for us to assimilate to it. What's more, this ruling centre props itself up precisely by resisting being the "other"—by not being the migrant, the Muslim and so on. In fact, even as they decry "segregation", their class politics ensures that it is more difficult to move an inch towards that centre: next year, through cuts in grants and teaching jobs, it will be many times harder for migrants to acquire English. We should of course support all resistant cultures whilst identifying ruling lies about their own desirable purity, and celebrating how we defy atomisation, segregation and oppression through all the many ways we mix.

◆ This article was first published in *Socialist Review*, April 2011

TWO POEMS BY MICHAEL ROSEN

The bus goes on and it's full and it's leaving and it's
laughing and it's going on and it's morning and it's
evening and it's in Punjabi and it's daytime and it's
full and it stops and it's suspicious and it starts and
it's in Ibo and it's shouting and it's shopping and
it's rapping and it's lit up and it's dark and it's shove-up
and it's crying and it's squealing and it's in Dutch and
it's braking and it's in Geordie and it's at the station
and it's skint and it's full of babies and it's full of men
and it's going on and it's past the Vietnamese café and
it's past the tyre depot and it's past the silver car and its
chauffeur and it's waiting for Sinatra to start up and it's
in patois and it's chips and vinegar and it's past the
park and it's full of football and it's a bellyache and it's
full of jokes and it's scared and it's in Arabic and it's
back from school and it's pushing and it's raining and
it's ripe armpits and it's tranks and it's angry and it's
full of yesterday and it's riding under the lights and it's
fucked off and it's the smell of oil and it's pissed and
it's combing and it's kissing and it's packets of rice and
it's cassava and it's over the canal and it's the baby's
bottle and it's over the railway and it's under the cranes
and it's in the shadows of the palaces in glass and it's
in Albanian and it's bleach and it's the homework in
late and it's spuds and it's the hijab and it's shoulders next
to backs next to fronts and it's revving and it's too late
and it's too early and it's not enough and it's going on
and it's on time and it's dreaming and it'll get there
today and it'll get there tomorrow

He said, I can't stand it any more, it's doing me head in.
This place used to be like a village.
—What's the matter with it? I said.
—It's full of foreigners, he said. I love
Walthamstow, he said, but I can't stay here.
I'm going.
I wondered where but I said nothing. He didn't say
anything else, so I said, Where to?
—Spain, he said.

Ruling Britannia:
Capitalism, class and culture

GARY MCFARLANE

Culture is often seen as a defining national characteristic—a definition of what it means to be who you are. The purpose of this article
is to show why this view could not be further from the truth.

In reality, human nature is in the first instance a struggle for food,
clothing and shelter. From that point flows everything else. Much of
that "everything else" is what we commonly call culture: the different
ways in which human beings have sought to understand and master the natural world—in other words the way we live. This process
is predicated on the social imperative that underlies all human activity: without working together to secure food, clothing and shelter we
wouldn't be here today.

From subsistence hunter-gatherer societies to today's all-conquering
capitalist societies, co-operation has been the hallmark. To co-operate
requires communication and it is the development of language that
most clearly demonstrates this obvious fact.

The popular view of culture as demarcated zones dividing masses
of humans from each other has more to do with the invention of the
modern nation state, with its borders and flags, than it does with
the reality of human history, both distant and more recent. Cultural
traits—from the food we eat, the clothes we make and wear, to the
architecture we imagine and create—are all, in the modern world, the
product of shared cultures. Even among the few tribal hunter-gatherer
communities that have not had the misfortune of succumbing to global industrial capital, the similarities between themselves and "others"
faced with similar environmental conditions again subverts the fanciful

notion of timeless monocultures only lately polluted by "outsiders". In addition to this, all these cultural traits are learned. There is nothing innate about liking particular food or speaking a particular language.

Human beings have always migrated, interacted and intermingled. Modern genetics has reinforced this affirmation of our shared common culture as human beings by scientifically tracing the incidence of genetic variation that allows for the mapping of the migration of the earliest humans out from Africa.

Against this background then, multiculturalism as a concept sounds like a truism—as all cultures derive something from others. The real question is why the differences between cultures became elevated to the level of supposed impenetrable opposites, with some cultures seen as incompatible with others, indeed mutually antagonistic.

Cultural difference can't be explained through the economics of migrating bands of humans alone. As societies became more advanced and were eventually able to produce more than was required to just survive, classes of specialists arose who didn't have to work in the fields and were able to justify this position either through brute force or, more commonly, as the guardians of scientific knowledge, cultural history and religious ritual. This class apart lived better than the rest of society. Certainly, they would share many cultural norms and practices but they also created their own culture, designed to put a wall between themselves and the rest.

It was the advent of capitalism that brought the question of "culture" to the front page. The rise of the modern nation state could not be successful unless all those within national boundaries, the ruler and the ruled, the boss and the worker, were unified by some kind of common outlook that could obscure the class differences and interests that existed.

Those with power worked to strengthen the novel nation state with the invention of its corollary, a "national culture". The 18th century philosopher Edmund Burke saw this national culture defining what he called "the spirit of the nation". For him this unifying ideology was "made by the peculiar circumstances, occasions, tempers, dispositions, and moral, civil, and social habitudes of the people, which disclose themselves only in a long space of time". There is a grain of truth in what he says, but essentially its purpose is to provide the foundation for a big dollop of make-believe. The cultural critic Terry Eagleton has recently put it more accurately than Burke: "Culture, after all, is what helps power grow roots".[1]

There is no better starting place to examine Eagleton's insight than in considering the birth pangs of the capitalist state in Britain. It was Karl Marx who, with eloquent precision, described how the industries of the 18th and 19th century sucked in labourers from Ireland and pitted them against the so-called native born workers. "Nationhood" was used as a tool with which to divide these workers one from the other, thereby weakening the fighting potential of British workers. Marx observed that,

> Every industrial and commercial centre in England now possesses a working class divided into two hostile camps... The ordinary English worker hates the Irish worker as a competitor who lowers his standards of life.
>
> In relation to the Irish worker he feels himself a member of the ruling nation and so turns himself into a tool of the aristocrats and capitalists of his own country against Ireland, thus strengthening their domination over himself.

Marx showed how this antagonism was fanned by "the press, the pulpit and the comic papers" in much the same way that the media does today. I've lost count of the number of erroneous and Islamophobic stories about Muslims that get passed off as news.

Irish people, the first to come under the heel of British imperialism, were also the first to experience the deliberate and conscious racism of the employing class, who, not satisfied with sucking wealth from the labour of the "native born" found an even cheaper supply of workers to staff their mills and build their canals. During the 1840s the number of Irish in Britain doubled to around 800,000—driven out of their own country by famine and across the Irish Sea to be worked to the bone for the growing band of industrialists. And when the going got tough for the capitalists, faced from time to time with "combinations" (early unions) and strikes or economic crises—they would ship Irish people in as cheap labour or strikebreakers, while at the same time rubbing their hands with glee at the scope for spreading disunity and hatred among English workers against their Irish brothers and sisters.

Let us now take a look at the cultural emblems that are seen as integral to the canon of "British culture", beginning with that hymn to British imperialism otherwise known as "Rule Britannia".

The history of the patriotic ode is inseparable from the outlook and interests of the bourgeoisie, as a look at some of its original mid-18th century lyrics (second to fifth verses) makes clear:

> The nations, not so blest as thee,
>   Must, in their turns, to tyrants fall;
> While thou shalt flourish great and free,
>   The dread and envy of them all.
>
>   "Rule, Britannia! rule the waves:
>   "Britons never will be slaves."
>
> Still more majestic shalt thou rise,
>   More dreadful, from each foreign stroke;
> As the loud blast that tears the skies,
>   Serves but to root thy native oak.
>
>   "Rule, Britannia! rule the waves:
>   "Britons never will be slaves."
>
> Thee haughty tyrants ne'er shall tame:
>   All their attempts to bend thee down,
> Will but arouse thy generous flame;
>   But work their woe, and thy renown.
>
>   "Rule, Britannia! rule the waves:
>   "Britons never will be slaves."
>
> To thee belongs the rural reign;
>   Thy cities shall with commerce shine:

Gary McFarlane

All thine shall be the subject main,
    And every shore it circles thine.

    "Rule, Britannia! rule the waves:
    "Britons never will be slaves."

Locked in a struggle to the death with the French and Dutch for commercial supremacy, the anthem was consciously penned as a battle cry for the Royal Navy—an institution held in high regard by the country's rulers (but not its common people who were press-ganged into serving on its ships in vile conditions). And when the verse attacks "haughty tyrants" its author (the poet James Thomson) has in mind the autocratic French royal family and their counterparts across Europe, in contrast to the reined-in and fundamentally broken "constitutional" monarchy allowed to continue in the wake of the English Revolution.

Its refrain, "Rule, Britannia! rule the waves", was an exhortation to the navy to go forth and conquer. At this point Britannia did not rule the waves, while the reference to slaves pointed up to another contrast: that between the mythical free Englishman as against those who were still burdened, slave-like, under the rule of princely tyrants. No distinction is made between those at the top and those at the bottom. "Britons" referred to all classes, but when Thomson writes, "Thy cities shall with commerce shine" it's clear the interests embodied by the poem-cum-song spoke to the industrialists—not the working people driven off the land into the disease-ridden city slums. "Rule Britannia" is unlikely to have been sung very loudly in the mills, and even less so in the factory system. Nevertheless, never being slaves was a laudable ambition that was intended to speak to the ordinary people, and did find an echo.

By the Victorian era, when Britain, with its empire, had become the indisputable master of the waves, the meaning of the words subtly changed by tweaking the grammar. Instead of an exhortation to rule the waves the fact of the imperial achievement was registered by taking out the comma and adding another Britannia and an "s" to rule so that "Rule, Britannia! rule the waves" becomes "Rule Britannia! Britannia rules the waves".

The provenance of "Rule Britannia" shines a light on the conscious attempts of the rich and powerful to forge a fake national unity behind their class. "Rule Britannia" wasn't so much a product of a shared culture as it was of a ruling class one, thrust down the throats of the "lower orders".

Raymond Williams, in his seminal book *Culture and Society*, provides us with a general summary of what's at work here: "Tradition is always selective, and there will always be a tendency for this process of selection to be related to and even governed by the interests of the class that is dominant".[2]

Many of the cultural artifacts taken as totemic of Britishness are, upon closer inspection, found to have originated beyond these shores. The royals are a case in point: they had to change the family name to Windsor during the First World War to hide their German origin. By all accounts Queen Victoria spoke her English with a German accent, which was not surprising (or a problem for internationalists) given that her parents were German.

The patron saint of England, St George, is unfortunately much in vogue these days with the flag wavers, but whenever you mention to said nationalists that the man was not British and in fact either came from present-day Turkey or historic Palestine, you are, more often than not, met with a disbelieving stare.

Fish and chips, another staple of the national mythology of Britain, also has a surprising history. By the late 19th century it was becoming the fast food of the day, beginning first in east London and then spreading to the working class districts of the rest of the country. Certainly potatoes, although of course not native to this part of the world, were known to provide sustenance to the poor, particularly in Ireland, but the practice of frying food, and in particular fish, was a novelty with origins elsewhere.

The clue lies in the roots of the Jewish population that found sanctuary from oppression in Russia and Eastern Europe in 19th century east London. It was they who brought the culinary tradition of frying fish with them. According to food writer Jay Rayner the first fish and chip shop was opened in the East End in 1860 by a Jewish man called Joseph Malin, and it was another Jewish man, Samuel Issacs, who went on to open "Fish Restaurants" across the south of England in the late 19th century. Just in case it wasn't obvious that this was the food of the working class, the authorities designated it an "offensive trade", citing the smells, and by implication the people too, associated with fish and frying. It continued to be regarded as such until the Second World War when it lost any stigma as it was one of the few foods not subject to rationing. The frying of chips is thought to have initially become popular around the same time as the fish frying, but appearing first in the heavily Irish working class districts of the north of England and Scotland, with the two traditions merging to give us fish and chips.

All this could merely be seen as an interesting piece of social history until you consider the widespread anti-Semitism that existed at the time. The parallel with the racist "smelly food" complaint of later times aimed at new arrivals is striking.

The monoculture imaginings of the early anti-multiculturalists are all so much puff, but how is it that our rulers today still feel the need to sustain these traditions in the face of modern realities, and why? The answer, as intimated above, lies in the specific historical needs of the new capitalist state and the industrialists it served.

Much of what 19th century high society had to say about Jewish and Irish people was regurgitated, with a little tweaking, in later times for other groups: they're not the same as us, they eat funny food, look different, are all criminals, and so on. Certain prejudices were reserved for definite groups. So Jewish people were at one and the same time rich and poor in the minds of anti-Semites. The Irish were labelled uncultured, brutish drunks. At the turn of the 19th century more Jewish people arrived as refugees from murderous pogroms in Eastern Europe and they became associated with radicalism. Between 1880 and 1920 nearly four million Jewish people emigrated to the West—and they were met with anti-Semitism. The word "anarchist" became synonymous with lower-class Jews in the same way that Muslims today are all seen as potential terrorists.

Racist organisations such as The Association for Preventing the Immigration of Destitute Aliens, formed in 1881, and the later British Brothers League (BBL), were created out of hatred towards the thousands of Jews who joined the industrial working class of this country.

Jewish and Irish people provided convenient scapegoats for the rulers of the day who wanted to deflect anger against themselves towards others. Although the roots of the racism that underlay the persecution of minorities can be traced back to the Atlantic slave trade—the idea of inherited characteristics marking out a section of humanity as inferior—its driver in the modern world is in the labour market and the competition for jobs that is forced upon workers. Time and again employers across the decades and across the globe have sought to divide and rule their workforces using this key weapon in their ideological armoury.

The question of culture in this context is not just about supposed differences between workers but also the difference the powers-that-be rarely talk about—their culture and ours. This is not the preface to a fruitless discussion about "high" culture versus "low" culture. Instead it highlights how much more we all have in common as working people, whatever part of the world we may originally have come from, and the very different cultural world inhabited by the Camerons and their banker buddies. I have more in common with a refugee from Somalia than I ever will with the millionaire parasites of the City.

"Britishness" has never been a packaging up of common cultural values, it has always been the imposition of the values of the ruler over the ruled. Everyone who enters the nation state is forced to assimilate. As Terry Eagleton argues, "A common culture in this view incorporates outsiders into an already established, unquestionable framework of values, leaving them free to practice whichever of their quaint customs pose no threat." A truly shared culture would be something different. Eagleton describes how, "a common culture in a more radical sense of the term is not one in which everyone believes the same thing, but one in which everyone has equal status in cooperatively determining a way of life in common".[3]

The British establishment knows all too well that playing the race card has served it well in the past and playing it today is historically consistent and depressingly predictable for that class. But there is also something perversely uplifting in their brazen and poorly-disguised racism in that it will, and is, forcing a reaction. There's another element that informs the thinking of our racist government: unity on our side delivers results at their expense.

Really-existing multiculturalism as opposed to the divisive fiction that passes for commentary on these matters in much of the media, means that we are in a much stronger position to drive back the racists, in all their forms—be it the EDL on the streets or the Conservative Party in their private members' clubs. A Gallup opinion poll in 2009 threw up some surprising results on British Muslim attitudes—surprising, that is, if you are taken in by the commonly held prejudices peddled about the community. The poll found that more Muslims than non-Muslims would prefer to live in a mixed neighbourhood (67 percent for Muslims and 58 percent for non-Muslims)—which of course runs contrary to the lies painting a picture of all Muslims as a group happy in its isolation and unwilling to integrate. It would be strange if there was not a yearning to integrate when you think about it rationally, shorn of any reference to the anti-multiculturalist mood music, because it is in the direct economic interest of all immigrant groups to assimilate in order to get on in society. Therefore, far from there being resistance to learning English among newer migrant communities, it is seen by them as essential. This explains why many are fighting to save educational provision of English for speakers of other languages; and incidentally exposes the deep hypocrisy and real motives of the government by attempting to wipe out any resource in this area.

"Workers of the world unite" is not an abstract slogan but goes to the heart of a socialist understanding of multiculturalism—we fight for the right to be different in order to bring about real equality; it's the culture of the many against the few the world over.

THE BRITISH BY BENJAMIN ZEPHANIAH

Take some Picts, Celts and Silures
And let them settle,
Then overrun them with Roman conquerors.
Remove the Romans after approximately 400 years
Add lots of Norman French to some
Angles, Saxons, Jutes and Vikings, then stir vigorously.
Mix some hot Chileans, cool Jamaicans, Dominicans,
Trinidadians and Bajans with some Ethiopians, Chinese,
Vietnamese and Sudanese.
Then take a blend of Somalians, Sri Lankans, Nigerians
And Pakistanis,
Combine with some Guyanese
And turn up the heat.
Sprinkle some fresh Indians, Malaysians, Bosnians,
Iraqis and Bangladeshis together with some
Afghans, Spanish, Turkish, Kurdish, Japanese
And Palestinians
Then add to the melting pot.
Leave the ingredients to simmer.

As they mix and blend allow their languages to flourish
Binding them together with English.
Allow time to be cool.

Add some unity, understanding, and respect for the future,
Serve with justice
And enjoy.

*Note: All the ingredients are equally important. Treating one
ingredient better than another will leave a bitter unpleasant taste.*

*Warning: An unequal spread of justice will damage the people and
cause pain. Give justice and equality to all.*

Part of their class:
Muslim working class
struggles in Britain

◆◆

HASSAN MAHAMDALLiE

One product of the demonisation of Britain's Muslims by those forces desperate to provide a scapegoat for the fallout from the "war on terror" and economic vandalism has been a concerted effort to separate them out from the rest of society, to make them seem "alien" and culturally distant—especially in the eyes of the wider working class.[1]

Many people, including some who consider themselves on the left, seem to want to put Muslims in historical cul-de-sacs that downplay their working class lives and heritage. Why should this be? Muslims have been living, working and struggling in Britain in increasing numbers for well over 100 years, with early settlements going back to the 1600s.[2] Other sections of the working class are assumed to have traditions of struggle. Muslims seem to have no history, radical or otherwise. In an attempt to challenge this distortion I have sketched out three periods in which Muslim workers have fought exploitation and oppression: the struggles of Arab and Somali seamen in Britain's ports during the period of colonialism, the first industrial struggles of Muslim workers following the Second World War, and the radical Asian youth movements of the 1970s and 1980s.

I have had to pick the Muslim "strands" out of the general narrative of "Black History". This is not easy because the principal works uncovering Black history in this country, inspirational as many are, were written in the 1980s when religious identity was regarded as subordinate to "racial" identities, reflecting the unified struggles against racism which had taken place. This is not an indication of neglect. Rather it is because Muslim workers until relatively recently did not see their religion as the defining part of their political identity.

1850-1945—The portside struggles of the Muslim seamen and their communities

The opening of the Suez Canal in 1869 marked the beginning of significant Muslim immigration into Britain. Ship owners from Europe began to employ migrants from Yemen and Somalia as unskilled labourers in the engine rooms. These Muslim sailors joined a floating multinational proletariat that had up to that point largely been populated by Indian "lascars". By the end of the 19th century small port communities were establishing themselves along key trade routes. Arabs could be found boarding in the dockside areas of Cardiff, South Shields, and to a lesser extent Liverpool and Hull. In Cardiff they joined other migrant workers from Africa, the West Indies, India, China, Malta, Greece, Italy, Germany and other countries. Portside licensed boarding houses and cafes sprang up to service the Muslim sailors, becoming hubs for welfare and community needs.[3]

Some seamen began to put down family roots. Women who married them would often convert to Islam and take a Muslim surname, to be passed on to their children as the families became members of the dockside working class population. Elaborate and colourful processions through the streets were organised to mark the major Muslim festivals.[4] Nevertheless Muslim seamen, like the other black populations, met with fluctuating levels of racism, hostility and prejudice.

Modern racism had developed as a justification for the slave trade. During the era of empire it explained the subjugation of the colonies. Prejudices founded on notions of biological superiority of the "white race" now mixed with assumptions of cultural superiority.

The British colonisation of Muslim majority countries gave the racism of empire an anti-Islamic twist. Humayun Ansari, in his recent history of Muslims, has written how the early 19th century saw the emergence in Britain of "a new sense of cultural superiority" with the decline of the Ottoman Empire that had once challenged Europe from the East.

The drive to unite British society, especially the working class, behind the imperial project inevitably had an effect on attitudes. A 1918 survey highlighted "race prejudice" as especially strong towards the colonised peoples. "Very little of this hostility was formed on the basis of personal contact; most of it was 'derived' from the process of imperialism".[5]

However, it would be wrong to assume that British workers were a homogenous racist bloc. The British working class movement also had a significant tradition of anti-racism. The London Chartists in the 1840s chose a black tailor, the ultra-radical William Cuffey, as their leader. In the 1920s the working population of Battersea elected an Indian Communist, Shapurji Saklatvala, as their MP. He stood alongside the black mayor of Battersea, John Archer.

The general racism was sharpened by local antagonisms in the ports, especially when scarcity of employment could set British seamen against their black and Arab counterparts. The migrant seamen were herded into close-knit slum areas around the docks, with a colour bar in jobs and housing that tended to keep them from integrating with the local population. It was the official and open policy of Cardiff council and estate agents to refuse "coloured" families housing outside of Butetown. Officials could argue that "coloured men who have come to dwell in our cities are being made to adopt a standard of civilisation they cannot be expected to understand. They are not imbued with moral codes similar to our own and they have not assimilated our conventions of life".[6]

Black and Arab seafarers faced a further obstacle in the generally hostile attitude that the trade unions had towards them. The seamen's unions sought to bar foreigners from trade union membership, until union leader J Havelock Wilson reversed it, seemingly just on the practical grounds that it was better to contain the foreign seamen inside the unions than give the ship-owners a free hand with them.[7]

The shipping bosses used pitifully paid lascars to undermine the wages of white seamen, but instead of the unions making a common front against the owners, they fell into the trap of seeing the lascars as competitors and easily duped tools of the bosses. So when the National Sailors' and Firemen's Union (NSFU—later to become the NUS) emerged from a major strike in 1911 part of its attack on the shipping owners was the accusation that they were discharging British seamen and replacing them with lower paid foreign hands.

In Tyneside a local newspaper illustrated how racism encouraged by economic competition could fuse with the cultural racism of empire: "No matter how bad conditions are aboard ship, Mohamed (who can live on the smell of an oily rag or a stick of incense for a week) will not complain, but a Britisher always does. This is why poor, puzzled, ostracised, uncomplaining Mohamed is given preference to Britishers".[8]

The outbreak of the First World War resulted in a sudden increase in demand for seamen but the situation altered again dramatically when the war drew to a close. Arab seafarers were hit by a double blow. They found themselves out of work, once more suffering pre-war racist hiring practices by the shipping lines. And they also faced hostile mobs of demobilised seamen accusing them of taking their jobs.

The antagonisms exploded into the "race riots" in the first half of 1919. The attacks have, paradoxically, to be seen in the context of the huge outbreak in class struggle that rocked the British ruling class that year. The 1917 Bolshevik Revolution in Russia had lit a flame across Europe and beyond. Workers returning from the trenches found, not a "land fit for heroes", but rising prices, unemployment and poverty. They rebelled with a massive wave of militancy, with an average of 10,000 workers on strike for every day of the year.

One of the strike leaders was the future Labour cabinet minister Manny Shinwell, then the leader of the British Seafarers' Union. He reckoned that he could poach members from a union if he could be seen to be more hostile to foreign seamen (particularly Chinese lascars). At a strike meeting in Glasgow, Shinwell urged that "action should be taken at once" against the Chinese. A few hours later a racist gang attacked West African seamen.

The threat to the British ruling class lessened as 1919 unfolded and there was a decline in class confidence, especially among the least organised sections of the workers. As this happened, there was a repeat on a nationwide scale of the scenario Shinwell had more or less purposefully brought about in Glasgow, with some white workers attracted by the possibility of "kicking down" those worse off than themselves.

Blacks and Arabs were set upon in all Britain's major ports and suffered savage beatings, fire bombings and murders. In February the violence erupted in South Shields, in April in the London docks; in May it hit Liverpool and Cardiff in June. The intensity of the violence seems to have increased at each stage. In Cardiff the rioting lasted several days and resulted in three deaths.

Black and Arab seamen never took these attacks lying down, even when they were outnumbered. One account from the 1919 riots tells how a Somali imam, Hadji Mohammed, "was prepared to face the mob, but his white wife pleaded with him, so he clambered up a drainpipe, hid on the roof and watched his residence being reduced to a skeleton".[9] A white racist was killed on the first night of the race riot in Cardiff. One historian writes that "the police protected the main black settlement around Loudoun Square (Because they feared the blacks would kill more whites if they didn't) but left unguarded a secondary area of largely Arab settlement nearer the city centre. This population moved into Butetown for self-protection".[10]

In Liverpool black seamen had defended their boarding houses against a police raid. One policeman was shot in the mouth, another in the neck, a third was slashed on face and neck, and a fourth had his wrist broken.[11] Soon afterwards a West Indian, Charles Wotten, escaping police clutches after one raid, was cornered by a crowd of 200 to 300 racists who threw him into the docks and pelted him with stones until he drowned.[12]

1919-1950—The seamen and the inter-war years

The reaction of the authorities to the mob violence was to further crack down on the Muslim seamen. Arab and Somali sailors were reclassified from their previous status as British passport holding workers to unwelcome and problematic "aliens". In 1921 the Cardiff town clerk recommended that destitute seamen "be repatriated forthwith, or accommodated in a concentration camp",[13] and in 1922 hundreds of Adenese were repatriated out of the city.

The government issued new restrictions in 1920 and then 1925 under the Aliens Act which had been targeted in the first place against poor Jewish immigrants:

Horrible histories: Myths of tolerance and nationhood

All coloured alien seamen were henceforth to be registered with the police and to carry an identity card marked "SEAMAN" in red ink bearing a photograph and a thumb-print. It was argued that the last was necessary because it was more difficult to tell coloured men apart and some more positive means of identification was needed![14]

The NUS was granted the sanction in 1930 that Arab and Somali sailors specifically should be picked last (if at all) and go on a forced rota that meant they had to take any job offered them if they were not to lose their right to stay in Britain. Soon Somalis, Arabs and their families were pushed into starvation and destitution.

The seamen responded to the attack by launching a militant campaign to smash the rota, picketing shipping offices and lobbying to get the union's position changed. The violent confrontations that took place in Cardiff and South Shields as a result ended with Arab and Somali sailors being prosecuted and receiving "exemplary" sentences. They looked to radical forces to help them.

In Cardiff they were drawn into an alliance with the Communist Party and the bodies it influenced. One historian tells how "the International Transport Workers Federation sprang to the defence of coloured men in one of the perennial conflicts over national insurance. The following year black men were involved in a movement to increase wages within the NUS." As Neil Evans has written in his meticulous study of the period, "Butetown was viewed by the Communist Party at the time as one of the most productive areas to hold corner street meetings and sell literature. In the late 1930s the Colonial Defence Association led protest marches and deputations about relief scales to the City Hall in Cardiff".[15]

The Second World War—Shipboard militancy and early industrial roots

Labour shortages with the outbreak of the Second World War strengthened the position of lascars. They were in demand once again, but they were not prepared to put aside their maltreatment.

As historian Rosina Visram has written:

Three days into the war, by September 1939, as many as eight ships were on strike, Indian seamen demanding, in some cases, a 200 percent wage rise, including essential provisions like soap, warm clothing and bedding... The Board of Trade was forced into negotiations, enlisting the help of the India High Commissioner, Sir Firozkhan Noon, to act as mediator in order to minimise concessions.[16]

Meanwhile employment was opening up in another sector—the war industries, drawing in ex-seamen and new migrants, especially from pre-partition India (Indians, Pakistanis and Bangladeshis). Visram describes how:

Factories and war-related industries in London and Glasgow, but particularly in the Midlands, needed labour. Indeed, demand was so high that even their lack of English language was apparently no longer considered a handicap... Some gave up peddling [a trade traditionally occupied by Indian men] for more secure factory employment... The two most numerous ethnic groups engaged in industries in wartime Britain were Bengali Muslims, largely ex-seamen, and Punjabis, both Sikh and Muslim.[17]

By April 1943 there were up to 2,000 Indians labouring across Birmingham and Coventry.[18] Although they filled a crucial gap in the war industries, they were, as before, crowded into poor accommodation and faced discrimination at work. They responded by starting to organise themselves, socially, politically and through the trade unions.

The Indian Workers Associations (IWAs) had their origins in 1937, formed by Sikh activists living in Coventry with political connections to the Indian independence movement in Punjab, and by 1942 branches also existed in Birmingham, Bradford, London and other towns, with Sikhs, Hindus and Muslims joining together. The IWA's early activity was heavily influenced by Indian socialist and communist organisations, and branches and individuals had close political and membership links to the Communist Party. The secret service described a founder member, Coventry-based Akbar Ali Khan, known as the "driving force" behind the IWA, as holding "advanced political views".[19] Another founder member was Udham Singh, who became a martyr when he was hanged in Pentonville Prison in 1940 after shooting dead the colonial governor of Punjab responsible for the 1919 Amritsar Massacre of unarmed civilians (an incident featured in the epic film *Ghandi*).

Making their mark—post-war migration, new workers, racism and the industrial struggles

After the Second World War renewed migration from the colonies boosted Muslim populations in many parts of Britain. As a commentator observed in the mid-1970s, "migrant workers are used largely to fill jobs that native workers will not do, because of their low wages or low esteem. And yet they are jobs which are essential to the maintenance of public services that bolster our consumer economy".[20] Workers from the Indian subcontinent made up the majority of Muslim migration during this period.

The IWAs as a movement had faltered in the period after the Second World War[21] but revived in the late 1950s as Indians, including Muslims, faced other challenges. The Southall IWA, for instance, went from a membership of 120 in 1957 to 12,500 by the late 1960s. The branches gave a militant edge to community organisation, meeting welfare, social and cultural needs along with trade union and political leadership.

Historian and commentator Dilip Hiro noted, "Without exception, IWA members supported whatever militant action was taken by established unions in factories and public transport because they believed that the economic lot of Indian workers was intimately intertwined with that of British workers".[22]

Immigrant workers, although doing long hours of shift work for poor pay, were not in peripheral sectors of the economy: 43 percent of black workers in the mid-1970s were in factories employing over 500 workers, compared to 29 percent of white workers. And 61 percent of male black workers were unionised compared to 45 percent of white male workers.[23]

They were soon to move into confrontation with the employers, and often with racist union officials.

In May 1965 the first significant post-war "immigrant strike" took place at Red Scar Mill in Preston, Lancashire, involving Indian, Pakistani and African-Caribbean workers. It was opposed by the local TGWU organisation that characterised it as "tribal".[24] In May 1972 Pakistani workers struck at Crepe Sizes, Nottingham. Asians struck at Harwood Cash Lawn Mills in Mansfield and at EE Jaffe and Malmic Lace in Nottingham, and at Perivale Gütermann in Southall, west London.

What then was the industrial and political background to this rash of strikes and the race and class dynamics within them?

In 1962 the Tory government passed the openly discriminatory Commonwealth Immigrants Act. Harold Wilson's Labour government further turned the screws in 1965 and then in 1968 bowed before the racist hysteria unleashed by Enoch Powell to rush through parliament a law to block Asians with UK passports coming to Britain when they were driven out of East Africa. Further waves of racist hysteria accompanied the plight of Ugandan Asians in 1972 and Malawi Asians in 1976.

Those who did get through the barriers settled predominantly in London and the Midlands. East African Asians, whatever their previous status or profession, found only badly paid textile factory work open to them. Their entry into the manual workforce coincided with a weakening of the long post-war boom and disillusion with the Labour government. Although many had arrived penniless, that did not mean they were prepared to be passive in the face of hostility. Asian workers' battles became part of a pattern of growing union militancy.

But alongside the rising level of struggle there was also an underbelly of racist scapegoating, exacerbated by the ability of the far-right to exploit disillusion with Labour. The response of important groups of Asian workers marked a shift in British trade union politics and its approach to immigrant workers. It was in June 1972 that the first of the series of major industrial confrontations involving East African Asians took place at Mansfield Hosiery Mill in Loughborough:

> The lowest paid workers, bar loaders, all of whom were Asian, asked
> for a pay rise and in October struck—against union advice. What

Horrible histories: Myths of tolerance and nationhood

underlay their anger was the refusal of management to train them as knitters (all the knitters were white). Other workers came out with the bar loaders, although the whites returned to work within a week, and the strike was only made official after Asian workers occupied the union offices. A return to work eventually took place when the Asian workers accepted that 30 of the 80 knitters' jobs be reserved for them.[25]

Mansfield Hosiery was followed by a larger confrontation at Imperial Typewriters in Leicester in 1974. This strike involved 400 mostly East Asians, lasted for four months and quickly became political, with the focus moving from the issue of wages to that of racism and democracy in the trade unions. The strikers, many among them young women, fought against open racism on the part of white union members and their leaders. They organised mass pickets, resisted intimidation by National Front thugs, held three mass rallies, won widespread support inside and outside the local Indian community, and appealed successfully to the TGWU national leadership for an inquiry into the lack of Asian representation on the factory shop stewards committee.

The challenge to the trade union movement reached its height at Grunwick's two years later. The workforce at this film-processing factory in north west London was 80 percent East African Asian. In August 1976 nearly half of them walked out demanding union recognition. The ensuing strike was to last two years, with the trade union movement, black community and radical organisations and the left on one side and George Ward, the Anglo-Indian boss, the courts, the police and the forces of the organised right on the other.

The inspirational leader of the strike was the late Jayaben Desai, its secretary Mahmood Ahmad. He received a standing ovation after he told a meeting of 2,000 trade unionists at a British Leyland that TUC promises of real support were so much hot air. "If the British trade union movement wants to recruit Asian workers then it has to do better than this," he said.[26]

But if the top of the trade union movement was failing the Grunwick strikers, that accusation could not seriously be levelled at the rank and file. According to the "official" account of the dispute, a mass picket of the plant "transformed the strike":

It was the arrival in Willesden of thousands of trade unionists from all over Britain which was to reassure the strikers that they were not, after all, alone and that besides the right wing section of the labour movement there was also a left wing, a radical and a militant section which responded with class feeling to the call of all workers in struggle, whether male or female, manual or clerical, black or white.[27]

While problems of racism continue in many workplaces and even some trade unions, Grunwick laid the ghost of black and brown workers being prepared to "undercut" whites and resist joining unions. And gone forever was the image of passive, "traditional", Asian women. It paved the way for a new black presence inside the union structures. The TGWU union, which had been the union of choice for Asian workers despite the position of many local union leaders, would go on to elect Bill Morris as the first black trade union general secretary in 1991.

In the battles that raged, from the Red Scar Mill strike to Grunwick, Muslim workers were among those actively involved in some of Britain's most militant strikes. It is not what set Muslim workers apart that stands out from an analysis of this period; rather it is what they had in common with others.

The Asian youth movements—radicalisation and the fight against racism and fascism

The radicalism of the late 1960s and early 1970s had its effect on Muslim and other black and Asian workers in Britain, especially on the younger generation of Asians confronted by the rising threat of the National Front (NF). In 1976 the NF polled 15,000 votes in Leicester, against the backdrop of a racist campaign against the entry of Malawi Asians to Britain. A series of racist murders followed. In Southall, west London, a young man, Gurdip Singh Chaggar, was struck down by a gang of drunken racist white youths. A leading fascist and Blackburn councillor, John Kingsley Read, celebrated the murder with the notorious phrase "One down, one million to go".

The Southall Youth Movement was one of many youth organisations born out of the necessity to defend the community. It considered itself more radical than the "old guard" connected with the IWAs. Many members of the youth movements had moved in and out of Trotskyist organisations, and although some later ended up hostile to the far left, there is no doubt that they were influenced by its politics and methods. The success of mass mobilisations against the National Front was followed by the founding of the Anti Nazi League and Rock Against Racism. The strategy of building mass organisation and direct action dominated the political culture that the youth movements were a part of.[28]

Youth groups were established in all over London and in Luton, Nottingham, Leicester, Manchester, Bradford, Sheffield and Birmingham and elsewhere.[29] The Bangladeshi Youth Movement in Tower Hamlets was organised in response to the racist murder of Altab Ali in Whitechapel.

These organisations had different ethnic and religious membership reflecting the geographical area which they operated from, but, as historian Anandi Ramamurthy has pointed out, they all "worked with white anti-racists".[30]

It was members of the Bradford Youth Movement who came to national prominence. In the summer of 1981 there were rumours that the Asian community was to be the target of an organised fascist attack. After the youth put in preparations for self-defence, police discovered petrol bombs on some waste ground. Twelve members of the Bradford Youth Movement were arrested and charged with conspiracy to cause an explosion and endanger lives.[31]

"The Bradford 12" were put on trial a year later, prompting a huge campaign. Over half of the defendants came from Muslim families.[32] Their lawyers ran what was seen as an audacious defence—rather than lodge a guilty plea they would argue that the 12 had been acting in legitimate self-defence and in defence of their communities. The jury agreed and acquitted them.[33]

Although the youth movements could incorporate and unify activists across different faith backgrounds, it would be a simplification to describe them as purely secular movements as their members often hold strong religious convictions.[34] Bradford 12 defendant Tariq Mehmood looking back explains that:

Most of the people in the youth movements were religious, but religion was not an issue for the members; it was their own affair. Many Sikhs, Hindus and Christians helped to protect mosques, as Muslims did of temples when they were attacked. We had very close relationships with gurdwaras and mosques. There were many among the Muslim [members] who kept all fasts... The unity was in anti-racism and anti-imperialism... Ishaq Mohammed Kazi came to me about the question of God. Two weeks later he was in jail as part of the Bradford 12... Any divisions were political, either Labour Party or left party. Or else caste or national.[35]

The youth movements went into decline through the 1980s, partly as a result of the general downturn in workers' struggles that removed a unifying outward-looking focus for Asian youth. Another weighty factor in their decline was the "carrot" dangled by substantial state funding of "community" resources and the consequent co-option of activists. This state funding was also increasingly organised on ethnic and religious lines.

The youth movements should be viewed in the broader sweep of the history of struggles of working class Muslims in Britain. From the courageous and radical struggles by the pioneering seamen and their families, through the tenacious and uncompromising struggles of the factory workers to the radical formations against fascism and racism, this is a history that anyone can be proud of. The future chapter in this narrative is already in the making.

◆ An early version of this essay was published in *International Socialism* 113 (2007) http://www.isj.org.uk/index.php4?id=288&issue=113

Imperialism and homophobia: going beyond "common sense"

◆◆

COLIN WILSON

In February 2011 the BBC screened a documentary about Uganda, *The World's Worst Place to be Gay?*, fronted by gay Radio 1 DJ Scott Mills. Mills documented the grim facts: serious attacks against lesbians and gays are going on in Uganda, with a bill under discussion in parliament which would introduce the death penalty for gay sex if the offender has previous convictions, is HIV+ or has sex with someone under 18. There is widespread public hostility to gay people, and gay activists face murderous attacks—such as that on David Kato, who was beaten to death in January.

The government of Malawi also received widespread publicity in May 2010, when Steven Monjeza and Tiwonge Chimbalanga—who was born male but identifies as a woman—were sentenced to 14 years in jail after being arrested at a traditional betrothal party. The couple were eventually pardoned after considerable international pressure. Homophobic attacks have also taken place in Muslim countries: in 2001 in Egypt 21 men were arrested at a nightclub in Cairo and eventually sentenced to three years jail for "habitual debauchery", while the government of Iran has also executed and publicly flogged lesbian, gay and bisexual people.

These facts are bad enough. What is just as worrying is the perception that has now become "common sense" for sections of the lesbian, gay, bisexual and transgender (LGBT) media and community— that African and Middle Eastern people are generally homophobic, while white Western Europeans are on our side. This is just too close to colonial style racism—whites are enlightened, non-whites are backward—for us to accept it. It fits all too well with Islamophobia against Muslims in this country, such as journalist Johann Hari's recent article in gay style magazine *Attitude*, in which he claimed that exactly zero percent of Muslims have positive views about gays. And it can give comfort to the English Defence League's claim that they support LGBT rights against Muslim homophobia.

The importance of these issues was underlined in early 2011 in east London. Stickers appeared in the streets in February referencing the Quran and declaring the area a "gay free zone"—later in the year an 18 year old Muslim man was convicted of a public order offence. Many people were rightly horrified by this homophobia, so when an East End Pride march was called it quickly gained widespread support. But some activists also raised concerns about the march's organisers: they were not known in the area, and some of their Facebook friends were EDL members. The EDL had previously attempted to organise an anti-Muslim march in Tower Hamlets, but been forced to cancel the event after it became clear they would face mass opposition from East End United and Unite Against Fascism.

In the following weeks local LGBT organisations such as Out East, Rainbow Hamlets and Imaan expressed their concerns about the march. LGBT campaigners in Tower Hamlets had established relationships with people from local faith groups—East London Mosque, for example, had made a statement condemning homophobia, as had Lutfur Rahman, the borough's Muslim mayor. Now they expressed fears that the march might turn Muslim and LGBT people against each other—particularly a risk in a deprived area like Tower Hamlets, at a time of public spending cuts—dividing the community and benefitting nobody.

Evidence was finally produced that Raymond Berry, one of the march organisers, had links to the EDL. Almost immediately the march was cancelled; its organisers have not been heard from since. This was an important victory for the idea that we fight both Islamophobia and homophobia most effectively through unity. However, some prominent LGBT figures, such as journalists Johann Hari and Paul Burston, took a different view: having supported the march, they criticised those raising questions as being soft on "Muslim homophobia".

The fact is that stereotypes about Muslims in the UK are entirely inaccurate. As with any group, some Muslims are homophobic—but most are not. Stonewall research has repeatedly found that religious people are no more likely to be homophobic than anyone else—and the group most likely to be prejudiced is not Muslims or people from ethnic minorities, but older white British men.

As far as international politics are concerned, we need to remember that the fight against homophobia in the UK is also far from over. While Scott Mills assured a group of men in a Kampala gay bar that "in England it's easy to be gay, everywhere it's allowed" and that he can be openly gay in any bar in London, the truth is less rosy. Ian Baynham was kicked to death in Trafalgar Square in 2009 by homophobic attackers. Stonewall figures suggest that each year one in eight lesbians or gay men are victims of hate crime. We've only had an equal UK age of consent since 2000, all sex between men was illegal in Britain till 1967, and 41 US states still ban gay marriage—it's absurd to talk about LGBT rights being an essential part of Western values.

Research by Stonewall, for example, shows that LGBT refugees frequently face appalling treatment from immigration authorities—they are expected to describe intimate and sometimes horrific experiences to officials without hesitation, only to have their sexuality questioned, or to be told to go back to their country of origin and live "discreetly". In May 2011, for example, Ugandan asylum seeker Betty Tibikawa was told that she would be deported. She had been attacked as a teenager in Uganda because of her sexuality by three men who branded her on the inner thighs with a hot iron, injuring her so badly she was confined to bed for two months. Since then she has been "outed" as a lesbian by a Ugandan magazine in February 2011, and has been disowned by her family.

We need a better understanding of international LGBT issues than the "common sense" one, starting with the nature of the international political order. We live in a world divided up into countries in competition with each other. In each country political and economic power is integrated—oil is a crucial commodity economically, for example, so the US uses its political and military power to try to gain control over oil reserves. In this system—which Marxists call imperialism—some countries have much more power than others. The US currently uses economic and military power to dominate the world: in the 18th and 19th centuries Britain and France controlled vast and brutal empires. The British Empire was originally built on Caribbean slavery, and its crimes included one million deaths in Ireland during the 1848 famine—during which the authorities continued to export food from the country—and killing thousands of Indians to suppress the Great Rebellion of 1857-58.

The main motivation for imperialism has always been control of territory, resources and trade. Columbus sailed to America by accident because he was looking for a trade route to China. But sexual oppression has frequently been part of the picture too: as early as Columbus's second voyage to America in 1495, the sailor Michele de Cuneo reported in a letter home that he had come across a beautiful Caribbean woman "and the admiral gave her to me".

Different attitudes to sex became markers of the relative worth of different cultures—British respectability was judged superior to more relaxed Asian or African attitudes. Anal sex between men was banned throughout the empire by the Offences Against the Person Act of 1861, creating a taboo which had not existed in many places till then. Because the non-European world was seen as an exotic, sensual place, it was also depicted as a European's sexual playground. Gauguin painted naked young women from the Pacific islands, while other painters depicted harems filled with luxurious furnishings and compliant sex slaves.

Nor was sexual subordination confined to art. In 19th century British India, for example, most ranks in the British army were not permitted to have their wives live with them. Instead the army authorities organised brothels where Indian women and girls, some as young as 12, provided sexual services for British troops. The memoirs of colonial administrators tell the same story: a 1950s British rubber planter in Malaysia recalled that he was provided with a female servant who cooked his meals and had sex with him.

This sexual playground was also open to men who sought sex with other men, if they could afford to travel there. British novelist E M Forster lost his virginity in Egypt in 1914 with another man. 1960s gay playwright Joe Orton took holidays in Morocco because teenage male prostitutes were available. These encounters reflected a general perception that Muslim countries were more accepting of sex between men than Christian ones. In the 1840s a Moroccan visitor to Paris wrote with surprise about French customs: "Flirtation, romance and courtship for them take place only with women, for they are not inclined to boys or young men. Rather, that is extremely disgraceful."

For the African and Asian independence movements which developed through the 19th and 20th centuries, sexual exploitation was an example of imperialism's moral bankruptcy. The great anti-colonial writer Frantz Fanon wrote in his book *The Wretched of the Earth* about sexual exploitation in the Caribbean, where "centres of rest and relaxation and pleasure resorts [are] organised to meet the wishes of the Western bourgeoisie". A concern for sexual dignity, a rejection of racist stereotypes of Asians and Africans as exotic and sexual, an end to exploitation—in particular, that of women—were thus all part of anti-colonial movements.

Activists in the nationalist movements were not typically the rural poor, peasants or workers, but middle class urban people. Generally men, they had been educated in schools run by missionaries, spoke English or French, and worked in professional, European-style roles as doctors, lawyers or civil servants. They felt that they were fitted to rule their "own" countries—a view which led them to oppose white colonialists, but also set themselves apart from the mass of the people.

Such leaders were concerned to show that they would make capable, respectable rulers. The end result of many anti-colonial struggles in the mid-20th century was that societies changed largely at the top—black rulers replaced white rulers, and while this was a real step forward, much of the existing structure of society was left intact. This separation from the masses was crucial to the attitudes nationalist leaders took to sexuality. Along with European concepts like the nation-state and modernisation, they accepted the ideas about sexuality which dominated Europe at the time. For example, Arab nationalist intellectuals in the 19th and 20th centuries argued that their society had been colonised because it had become decadent. To gain independence its national culture must be revived. But that national culture was now reinvented to fit European standards, and so, for example, poems by the great 9th century Arabic poet Abu Nuwas which mentioned the pleasures of boys and wine began to be left out of anthologies.

One final element in nationalist attitudes to sex is that most anti-colonial struggles were won in the mid-20th century. In this period the rapid economic development of the Soviet Union seemed an attractive model to many nationalist movements. Many nationalists were influenced by Stalinist politics, which provided an apparently radical alternative to those of their former colonial masters. But the Soviet Union was far from radical in any sense—including over homosexuality, which was illegal there.

This explains how ideas about sex which were typical of 19th century Europe came to be accepted in anti-colonial movements. But to give a more detailed picture of recent events in Malawi and Uganda, we have to look at some issues particular to Africa.

Like everywhere else on earth, pre-colonial African societies included sex between women and between men. An anthropologist in the 1950s reported that among the Iteso people of Kenya and Uganda "people of hermaphroditic instincts are very numerous". Still today there exist in parts of Africa traditions of hugging and kissing, and sometimes also sex, between young women. In 19th century Uganda, King Mwanga insisted that his pages have sex with him, as was traditional. They had recently converted to Christianity and refused: the king demonstrated his authority by executing 30 of them.

Yet it's common for Africans to assert—as they did repeatedly in the Scott Mills documentary—that homosexuality is non-African, a destructive European import. Such ideas go back, once again, to the colonial period, and attitudes that developed in different parts of the empire.

It was impossible for Europeans to deny that Asian history had included advanced civilisations. But since Europeans had now conquered them, they concluded that Asians must have become decadent, a decadence which included sexuality. So Europeans didn't deny that sex happened between men and between women in the Middle East or India.

Africa and the Pacific, meanwhile, were seen by the colonial powers as peoples without a history, living in a "state of nature"—primitive, but natural. Europeans used this idea to make both liberal

Horrible histories: Myths of tolerance and nationhood

and reactionary arguments. The anthropologist Margaret Mead, for example, claimed that Pacific people had a relaxed attitude to adolescent sexuality: by implication, this was natural, so Europeans and Americans should take the same approach. But the assumed "naturalness" of African sexuality also implied that Africans were incapable of "unnatural" same-sex practices.

Against this background, we can begin to understand the growth of homophobia, for example, in Uganda. Uganda is a poor and undeveloped country; one in three people live on less than $1 a day, and four out of five people work in agriculture. This is a legacy of empire: the role of a colony is to produce raw materials, not manufacture goods. Since the 1970s imperialism has further undermined African development through debt and privatisation. Since coming to power in 1986 Ugandan president Museveni has done nothing to resist such attacks: early in his first term he agreed to a structural adjustment programme with the IMF and the World Bank, privatising state enterprises for a pittance and cutting government spending. He became popular in Washington: in 1997 the US Clinton administration described him as a "beacon of hope" who ran what they called a "uni-party democracy". In fact he has remained in power thanks to the use of torture and intimidation of political opponents.

Promoting a homophobic panic suits Museveni. Scapegoating a minority diverts attention from his own corruption, and allows him to pose as a defender of a supposed traditional African culture against the corruption of Europe and America—when in fact he has worked hand in glove with global financial institutions and multinational companies.

The Christian right in the US has also played a major role in developing Ugandan homophobia. The *New York Times* reported in January 2010 that American evangelical Christians prompted the original introduction of the Anti-Homosexuality Bill by speaking at meetings involving thousands of Ugandans the previous year. They had spent three days telling audiences that gay people could choose to be straight and that homosexuality is linked to paedophilia.

The Anglican church in Uganda also has a poor track record: the Anglican priest at gay activist David Kato's funeral chose that moment to deliver a homophobic rant, Anglican bishops unanimously gave a standing ovation at a conference last year to anti-gay speakers, and the church has cut the pension of a retired bishop who opposes the Anti-Homosexuality Bill.

So Ugandan homophobia has developed in a context of poverty and lack of democracy, in which Western governments are complicit, and has been provoked and sustained by right wing Christians from the US, and others who are part of a church based in Britain. So it makes no sense for LGBT people in imperialist powers like Britain and the US to side with their governments against African and Asian governments. Nor does it help LGBT people in the countries concerned, since European interventions can help reinforce the claim that homosexuality is not part of African or Asian culture. British activists need to take particular care regarding countries like Zimbabwe, Jamaica, Uganda and Malawi, all former British colonies—for someone from Britain to complain about these countries' human rights record can look ridiculous to people living there, many of whom can remember the brutality of empire.

Second, attitudes will only really change in Africa or Asia if those changes are won by people in those countries. Of course, you can understand why LGBT people here are horrified when they see witch-hunts going on: they want to express solidarity and do what they can to help. But just as real change in Egypt and Tunisia only happened when people there fought back for themselves, so Western ideas, support or money aren't the main things that will bring change for LGBT people in Africa or the Middle East. Just as we fought to change attitudes here, rather than someone handing us our freedom, sexual minorities in other parts of the world must find their own way to liberation.

Such change is a concrete possibility. The end of apartheid in South Africa was won amid a near-revolutionary situation as huge strikes by black workers created social upheaval in which all accepted ideas were called into question. Gay members of the liberation movement came out—in some cases in prison, while facing a death sentence from the racist regime. The fact that LGBT people were part of the movement helped activists to argue that the new South Africa had to include justice for lesbians and gays as well as racial justice. Gay and lesbian rights were included in the 1996 constitution—a first for any country—and laws were passed which guaranteed equality in employment, in service provision and regarding civil marriage. In each of these areas equality was gained in South Africa before it was won in Britain.

These changes are a first step, and they can be reversed, but they make the key point that imperialism has created the context within which homophobia can grow. We fight for sexual liberation not by siding with the imperialists, but by forming part of the struggle against them.

Photo essay:
East London Mosque

◆◆

REHAN JAMIL

Horrible histories: Myths of tolerance and nationhood

Rehan Jamil

Horrible histories: Myths of tolerance and nationhood

Rehan Jamil

SECTION THREE

NEVER ON OUR OWN
UNITY MATTERS

◆◆

Muslims, multiculturalism and the politics of dissent

◆◆

SALMA YAQOOB

Editor: What has been the impact of David Cameron's attack on multicul-turalism in the Muslim communities?

Salma: The immediate impact is the personal feeling of being under attack simply for following a particular religious faith. It is a feeling that has become depressingly familiar.

When the Prime Minister says that "we have even tolerated these segregated communities behaving in ways that run counter to our val-ues",[1] everybody in the country knows it is Muslims he is referring to. The "we" that David Cameron talks of clearly does not include us. His speech gave credence to a view that is normally the preserve of the BNP and EDL; that there is something problematic about Britain's Muslim communities because there is something fundamentally "un-British" and sinister about us and the way we live our lives. It is a view increas-ingly echoed by mainstream politicians.

When the prime minister of the country speaks in such a way, it shifts the whole terms of the debate further to the right, and legiti-mises speaking about Muslims in really quite an extreme manner. And it was not an accident that Cameron's speech was made in Germany. I believe the Tories want to undermine Britain's multicultural model, with its emphasis on pluralism and mutual respect, and replace it with one more based on the German monocultural, assimilation model.[2]

I found Cameron's comments deeply hypocritical in a number of ways. On the one hand he criticises non-English speakers for not learning the language,[3] and suggests this reflects their unwillingness to integrate. On the other hand, his government has slashed funding to the very classes that enable people to learn the language. In 2011 alone, it is estimated that up to 100,000 people will lose the opportunity to attend English classes. In 2007, David Cameron visited the ward I represent, Sparkbrook in Birmingham.[4] He was on his quest to make the Tory party electable by shedding its "nasty" image. He stayed overnight with personal friends of mine; a Muslim family living in an area with a very large Muslim population.

Afterwards he spoke about the experience in very glowing and positive terms. He called for "a concerted attack on racism and soft bigotry". He described how "we cannot bully people into feeling British". He made it clear that "integration" was a two-way street in which we all had responsibilities. And he urged people to avoid using loaded terms like "Islamists" and "extremists" when speaking about Muslims. His visit was positive and his comments were a helpful contribution.

The most charitable interpretation of his lurch to the right is that he has bent to the pressure of the right wing of his party. I suspect, though, that we were pawns in his PR makeover. Now we are to be pawns in his exploitation of people's fear and insecurity.

Do you see any differences between the approach to British Muslims by the last government and that being taken by the Con Dem coalition?

I think there is a very strong continuity. They both claim to be "preventing violent extremism" while existing in a state of denial about its causes. Unless we understand the appeal of violent extremist ideologies, we will be fighting them with one hand tied behind our backs.

Both the New Labour and Tory governments have obstinately refused to acknowledge the extent to which anger over Western foreign policy is the fuel that sustains these extremists. This is not a new argument. The intelligence services pointed this out at the start of the Iraq war.[5] Rather than confront this reality, the focus is shifted to how "ideology" is undermining "identity". It is as if ideology existed in a vacuum, devoid of time and place.

Central to the arguments of both New Labour and the Tories is a claim that Britain's multicultural model is, at best, an incubator of separateness and division, and, at worst, an incubator of extremism and terrorism.

In many ways Cameron's latest attack on our multicultural society is only a continuation of the debate begun by New Labour, in which Trevor Phillips [the head of what was then the Commission for Racial Equality] argued that British society was "sleepwalking into segregation".

The good news for anti-racists is that the intellectual case for the Blair-Cameron argument has been conclusively trashed. Academics have shown that it is simply not the case that Britain's communities are becoming increasingly segregated as Phillips claimed in 2005.[6]

The bad news for anti-racists is that despite the real evidence of the strengths of multiculturalism, its opponents are very determined and vocal in repeating a narrative that promotes a negative view of our diverse society—one which fosters fear, suspicion and division, all in the name of being concerned about integration.

While I think there is some continuity between New Labour and Cameron, I fear that the Tories will go much further down this road. In a time of economic crisis the creation of scapegoats is the oldest trick in the book. I fully expect Cameron to play this card.

In recent times Muslims across Europe have been under a great deal of hostile scrutiny by the state, the media and racist political parties. Are things getting better or worse?

While each country has its own dynamic, it appears to me that the overall situation in Europe is getting worse. There are now strong echoes across Europe of the way that Jewish people were demonised in the early part of the 20th century.[7]

I think the situation is deteriorating here in the UK too. The Tory chairman Baroness Warsi was right when she stated that Islamophobia has become the acceptable face of racism.[8] And as that "polite" prejudice becomes increasingly commonplace, it has its reflection in the openly violent and hate-filled activities of the EDL.

The BNP are facing electoral oblivion after their hammering in the local elections. But I think there is a real danger of the government shifting even further to the right in an attempt to draw that constituency into its own orbit.

One of the biggest problems is the way this creeping racism infects public debate. I recently took part in an edition of BBC One's The Big Questions. The debate was titled, "Does Britain have a problem with Muslims?" I really don't think we would see a programme under the banner of "Does Britain have a problem with Jews?" or "Does Britain have a problem with Black people?" It is as if the clock has been turned back to a time when the "foreigner" was blamed for every social problem. There has been an enormous retreat even from basic standards of respectful discourse.

Muslims make up only 3 percent of the population so most people won't know any, or rarely come into contact with us. What they do know of us is largely shaped by the media. The journalist Peter Oborne was right when he stated that there is a "shameful Islamophobia at the heart of the British media".[9] One way it express itself is in the enthusiasm with which the right-wing media jump on every word and action from ridiculous figures like Anjum Choudary [leader of Islamist group Islam4UK], and help give the impression that he is in some way representative of the community.[10] He is not. He and his followers are totally marginal and are repeatedly denounced from within the community and indeed driven from places where they attempt to organise.[11] His actions unquestionably add fuel to an Islamophobic fire already burning brightly. They also serve to detract from a more accurate depiction of Muslims in Britain whose positive contributions become sidelined in the sensationalist reporting.

The space for Muslims to be vocal, to protest and dissent, especially against British foreign policy and military interventions, without being branded as extremist seems to be under threat. Is this your experience?

When Muslim public figures dissent, especially when it comes to opposing our government bombing our Muslim brothers and sisters abroad, we invariably are subject to vilification and demonisation.

I had direct experience of this recently when myself and a Respect party colleague refused to join other councillors in applauding a soldier who had returned from Afghanistan, even though they refused to hold any debate on the war itself in the council chamber. I personally contacted the soldier and released a public statement to make clear my action was not directed against the soldier as an individual, but against the politicians who refuse to hold our government to account for a decade of failure in Afghanistan, while shedding crocodile tears about those who return from this war injured, maimed or worse.

The issue was seized on by a leading local Liberal Democrat politician, who received huge publicity for attempting to portray me as an Islamic extremist. He said: "If Councillor Yaqoob had her way, she would be implementing Hadood Law, with hands cut off and stonings... I can only assume that if one of the failed 21/7 London suicide bombers had been in the council chamber, Councillor Yaqoob would have been demanding the council applaud the failed suicide bomber for their past heroic actions".

For at least a week this story featured prominently in the media in Birmingham, and was picked up nationally. It is an interesting case study of exactly the kind of vilification Muslims face if they dare speak out.

It did not matter that the attacks on me were complete lies. Even a cursory glance at my record would consign any such charge to the dustbin. I have openly and repeatedly condemned terrorism.[13] I have spoken out in favour of women's rights;[14] I have spoken out against anti-Semitism;[15] I have argued against homophobia[16] and all forms of oppression.

Facts were irrelevant. The intention is to smear. One feature of our world since 9/11 is the way that Muslims who criticise our foreign policy invariably find themselves described as "extremists". The term is most often used in a cynical and sinister way, intended to smear political opponents. It acts to blur any difference between Muslims critical of government policy but who advocate engagement in the political process to change it and Muslims who abhor any such engagement and advocate violent, sectarian alternatives. This is an ugly politics, and the politicians who practice it are playing a dangerous game.

Its effect among non-Muslims is to feed a sense of fear, intolerance and racism towards Muslim communities. Its effect on Muslims is to play directly into the hands of those within the community who argue that there is no place in British society for any Muslim who cares about their brothers and sisters abroad; that they will always be viewed as a "suspect community"; that they will never be treated equally.

Interestingly, the soldier in question said there would not have been the same hue and cry if it had been non-Muslims councillors involved, and his comments helped turn the issue around. In the end the Lib Dem councillor was forced to issue a public apology fearing a reprimand by the Standards Board. It was a moral victory, but by then considerable damage had been done.

The larger point is this: for all the talk about Muslims and identity, once we exercise our citizenship rights and freedom of speech we find all too quickly our very citizenship being brought into question.

What has been the effect of the government's Preventing Extremism programme on our Muslim communities and the way they are perceived by wider society?

The record of the first Prevent programme was not good. In fact it was pretty much a complete waste of tax-payers' money. Unfortunately, the re-launched Prevent strategy threatens to be worse. The original idea was to allow councils to channel money to local projects in the hope that would prevent Muslim youth from being drawn into a world of dangerous extremism. The experience in Birmingham was that while money was going to many worthwhile projects, none of them were really doing anything in terms of undermining the attraction of religious extremism.

For many of those seeking funding, Prevent was a gravy train. Worse, the way the scheme was set up it understandably drew resentment from other communities who felt their projects were cash-starved but could see funding available for ill-conceived projects targeting the Muslim community.

The big problem with the whole strategy is the way that all Muslims are treated as suspect, until we prove our suitability for "engagement" with government. This is obviously very different from an approach that is specifically hostile only to those with violent—and therefore illegal—agendas.

Rather like the Irish in the past, the Muslim community today is treated like a "suspect community". And inside the Muslim community there is both compliance and resistance. We had an example of this recently in Birmingham where the council and police attempted to introduce a ring of special spy cameras in Muslim areas. In areas where there was a tradition of political dissent, whether in mobilisations for the anti-war movement or voting for political alternatives, the resistance was strongest. Where there was no such tradition, there was practically no organised opposition. Thankfully, we had a strong enough base in Sparkbrook from which to mount a campaign to kill the scheme.[18]

This victory has national implications. If they had got away with it in a Respect party stronghold, they would have felt they could get away with it anywhere. What was encouraging about our campaign against "Project Champion", as it was called, was the solidarity from non-Muslims, determined not to allow their Muslims neighbours to be demonised.

It is this kind of engaged, democratic, opposition that the new Prevent strategy threatens to undermine. In its place would be a subdued population, unwilling to risk speaking out, particularly in situations where our government had gone to war in our name.

The new Prevent strategy takes a further turn for the worse by linking extremism to a contest of "values".

Framed in this manner, the debate can only go in one direction—towards the restriction of civil liberties. France is a case in point where restrictions have been imposed on the rights of Muslim women to wear the hijab and the denial of their right to wear the niqab for supposedly being at odds with French republican values.

There is no doubt that conservative interpretations of Islam may well clash with secularism, but it is dangerous to conflate debates about secularism and religion with those about anti-terrorism.

Surely the issue is not whether you or I share the same view on "values" but whether we seek to impose our differing values on each other. There are many divisions that run through all societies and many that revolve around deeply held beliefs or values. What is dangerous in the approach of this government is to assume the right to decide which is the "British" side of any argument, and which is "foreign".

The involvement of a range of "stakeholders", from lecturers to GPs to mental health professionals, in identifying "vulnerable" individuals is very sinister.

Nobody would expect their GP to be evaluating their political views, and submitting reports on how "extremist" they suspect them to be. They are not qualified to do such a thing, and involving health professionals in such activities deeply compromises their relationship with all their patients. But now, apparently, teaching, health and other professionals are to be cogs in the security apparatus.

The implications for civil liberties, and the integrity of some of our key institutions, are wide-reaching.

I agree with the comments of academic Richard Jackson[19] that the aim of the Prevent strategy, past and present, is to produce "docile subjects"; people who will just accept British foreign policy, whether out of fear or self-censorship.

The entire report is steeped in double standards and hypocrisy. We get lectured about violence from a government only too keen to use violence to pursue its own political goals around the world. We are supposed to take seriously comments about "democracy" and "civil rights" from politicians who go to war despite the will of the people, and collaborate with regimes using torture.

The report has more than a touch of Orwellian "thought-crime" about it. There is nothing inherently "extremist" about opposing imperialism, wanting to live in an Islamic homeland, or wanting to dress in a burqa—any more than it is "extremist" for people to wish they could dump capitalism and replace it with a communist or socialist society. These ideas only become dangerous to broader society if violent means are pursued to advance them.

We need more democracy, not less. There are genuinely dangerous extremists, and their appeal is strengthened by a feeling that political protest is pointless. The stronger our democratic protest movements are, the weaker the pull of these extremists.

When we built a peaceful, democratic and multicultural anti-war movement, we provided a strong answer to those extremists who wanted to exploit that anger for violent and sectarian purposes. Without that vigorous protest movement I do believe that the threat from Al-Qaeda politics would have been all the more serious.

The government quite rightly states that a sense of belonging is integral to ensuring that violent extremists are defeated. Yet, in seeking to restrict freedom of expression within the Muslim community, and in feeding a sense of suspicion and fear about the Muslim community, they play into the hands of the real extremists by undermining that very sense of belonging.

Since 9/11 Muslims in the UK have been viewed by those in power through the prism of the "war on terror". Is this also the way Muslims are viewed by the wider community you represent as a local politician, or are there perhaps different, more positive, stories to tell?

Muslims certainly have a PR problem! The negative narrative about us needs to be countered. But there are lots of good stories out there about communities that are working, and Muslim and non-Muslims living side-by-side in harmony. For example, the ward I represent faces major challenges of poverty. Yet despite this, in all the indices of community engagement we are thriving.[20]

A recent survey commissioned by Birmingham council questioned residents across the city on their attitudes to living in their neighbourhoods. On each of the following questions, Balsall Heath in my area came top: do you feel safe in your area? Do you feel proud of it? Do you trust people in your street? Do you trust the police? Do you trust the council? Do you feel able to influence events in your area? Quite remarkable, considering that it ranks among the five poorest wards in the country.

But not so surprising when you see the very many activities that bring residents together as neighbours, working to improve their shared area. All this has not come about in response to government finger-wagging but through patient work over many years on the ground by residents themselves.

We have challenges to face, of course. The 70 percent cut to our youth service budget that the ruling Conservative-Liberal Democrat administration has introduced will do more to unpick community cohesion than any threat of hate-spewing Muslim bigots.

Our story is the dominant story and the lived reality of the vast majority of Muslims. But it is a story which needs to get told more.

Contrary to the suggestion that we are all spongers, Muslims contribute £31 billion to the British economy.[21] The contribution of immigrant labour, including from South Asian communities, to the rebuilding of Britain after the Second World War is too often forgotten. As is the fact that of the 3 million volunteer soldiers from South Asia who helped British and Allies in the First and Second World Wars, over 1.1 million of them were Muslim.[22] Contrary to the idea that our "loyalty" should be questioned, poll after poll shows that Muslims have a higher levels of identification with Britain than non-Muslim communities;[23] and contrary to the suggestion that Muslim youth are all alienated a recent study from Lancaster University showed that young British Muslims are less radical, do better in school and suffer less discrimination than Muslim youngsters brought up in France and Germany![24]

Although our contribution to this country is not often recognised, there is nowhere else I would rather live. There are values of democracy, human rights, freedom of speech, pluralism and diversity which are embedded in the British people, if not always in our governments, which have been fought for, and are precious and appreciated. As studies show, these values are supported by vast majority of British Muslims. To talk of us having to fit into these values is misleading—we already do, and in some ways, even more so than other communities. For all the problems, Britain is good society for Muslims. I acknowledge that, and that's why I choose to bring my kids up here.

How important is the role of the trade union movement in combating anti-Muslim racism and encouraging unity across all our communities?

The Trades Union Congress (TUC) and the Muslim Council of Britain (MCB) have agreed a joint initiative to specifically challenge racism, to highlight the positive contribution of the TUC within the Muslim community and address the wider socio-economic problems that Muslims face.[25] This is a very important development, but much more work needs to be done to turn fine words into action.

We need more prominent figures in the Labour and trade union movement to defend and celebrate Britain's multicultural model and challenge this myth that it promotes separateness and division when the opposite is actually the case.

More generally, the more the unions fight the cuts, the more they are able to unite communities affected by the cuts—as long as it is done on the basis of addressing the concerns of all communities affected together. There is a danger that in a time of recession an "anti-immigrant" discourse can take hold. As people face insecurity about their jobs and homes, it is very easy for what is an economic issue to be racialised, and for communities to be turned against each other.

I was alarmed when Gordon Brown appeared to take this ground with his comments about "British jobs for British workers", and I am alarmed that the reconstituted Blairites of Blue Labour are attempting to revive the same slogan. I hope the trade unions resist pandering to these arguments because they simply give succour to those with scapegoating politics. Any such move would actually weaken the anti-cuts campaign as the focus would be shifted away from the flawed economic and ideological basis of the cuts which need to be challenged robustly.

Already the pro-cuts ideologues have achieved a propaganda coup of implanting in the public mind that cuts are inevitable and necessary because irresponsible public spending is the cause of the deficit.

Similarly much of the discomfort and insecurity experienced by those on the receiving end of cuts is being shamelessly blamed on multiculturalism and the language of identity is used as a convenient distraction from the real causes. The TUC's magnificent anti-cuts demo in March 2011 was a wonderful start in building resistance to the cuts. We need to build on it in a way that strengthens solidarity between all communities.

We need to build political alliances to defend the principles that our multicultural society is built on, what strategies do you think we should explore to that end?

Instead of "muscular liberalism" we need "muscular multiculturalism"! Multicultural Britain works. In a recent study researchers from the University of Manchester showed that neighbourhoods with higher ethnic diversity are associated with higher rates of social cohesion, respect for differences, and neighbours of different backgrounds getting on well together.[26] Strengthening the ties that bind us is the key to rolling back those who seek to undermine us.

I am really heartened when I see Sikh activists organising against the EDL;[27] or when Muslims defend gay rights and oppose women's oppression; or when the Jewish community speaks out against Islamophobia and Muslims do likewise against anti-Semitism. We cannot allow different communities to be pitted against each other. And, where possible, we must try and present any struggle for our specific concerns as Muslims in a way that upholds broader civil rights.

For example, in arguing for the right of Muslim women to wear the hijab, we must also uphold the rights of those who do not want to wear a hijab. The issue of the wearing of Islamic dress is not just about religious freedom; it is also about a woman's right to wear as she chooses. So, just as I support protests against the imposition of bans on Islamic dress for women, so too do I support those women organising the "slut-walks". They are different angles of the same argument: it's a woman's right to dress how she wishes. Central to effective anti-racist campaigning has to be building the broadest alliances.

If a campaign against Cameron's "muscular liberalism" and in defence of multiculturalism is left to the Muslim community alone, it will fail. If it is confined to sections of the Muslim community and the left, it will fail. The dividing line in forging the unity we need to roll back the coming assault is not whether you agree or disagree with the wars in Iraq, or Afghanistan or Libya.

Yes, the world post 9/11 massively accelerated the growth of Islamophobia, but it was a train that had already left its station in this country before 9/11; picking up passengers after the Rushdie protests [against his book The Satanic Verses] and northern riots along the way. The first real critique of our multicultural model stems from the period before 9/11, with the claims that the British model was fostering separateness between communities.

The dividing line instead must be whether you are for Cameron's "muscular liberalism", and his attempt to destroy the British model of multiculturalism, or whether you are against that. I think there will be many people from across the political spectrum who are alarmed about Cameron's attempts to shift race relations in this country along more European lines. For all the rhetoric of "citizenship" that accompanies it, the experience of the attack on multiculturalism in Europe has been to make minorities feel less like equal citizens, less belonging, to increase intolerance, anti-Muslim racism and feed the growth of the far right.

There will be many across the political spectrum who value Britain's tradition of respect and tolerance for difference and be alarmed at any attempt to undermine it. We must seek to make alliances with such people. Within those alliances and on public platforms we should make the connections between the so-called "war on terror" and Islamophobia.

And we should make connections between the cuts and the attack on multiculturalism. I think there is an ugly cynicism in the way this government is now talking about race as they seek to implement savage cuts on the most deprived communities. We should point that out and back it up with the fact that researchers from University of Southampton found that poverty and gross inequality are six times more likely than ethnic diversity to cause British people to be suspicious of their neighbours, "repudiating the argument that multicultural societies make people uneasy and less trusting of strangers".

Being centrally involved in fighting the cuts is critical, and not just from the viewpoint of preserving our few crumbs from the table, but in the interests of all. Cameron is partly right when he says "we are all in it together". With the worst of the cuts yet to come, and with a Tory government seeking to do to the welfare state what Thatcher could only dream about, the working class is in it together. It is the poorest third in society that these cuts will fall the heaviest on and it is this section that has the strongest vested interest in building resistance. However, establishing consensus on either the war on terror or opposition to the cuts cannot be the starting point in building the kind of campaign we need to fend off this new attack.

I think we can mount a large and effective campaign against this new attack on Muslims and multiculturalism generally.

I was struck by a speech given by Peter Oborne, the chief political commentator for the Daily Telegraph (and on everything else a solid Tory supporter), who has come out strongly against Cameron's "muscular liberalism" on the grounds that it erodes traditional British liberal traditions of respect and tolerance.

The trouble with inferring that "they" have different values to "us" is that it fosters ignorance, suspicion, and fear about those viewed as "them". It encourages intolerance.

And this intolerance has no limits. Once out, it can be a difficult genie to put back in the bottle. The wild and intolerant attacks on Muslim "values" have already led to a violently racist movement which targets all Muslims. But this intolerance has wider implications. It undermines the fundamental freedoms of all of us to live our lives, peacefully, in the ways that we choose for ourselves.

That is an issue that can unite a very wide range of people who value diversity and tolerance.

Understandably, the Muslim community feels quite isolated at the moment. It doesn't have to be.

The English Defence League:
The organ grinders' monkey

◆◆

MARTIN SMITH

Europe's leaders are using racism to draw attention away from their austerity measures. If they are the organ grinders then in this process they are legitimising the "monkeys", the racist and far right parties which are flourishing across much of Europe.

In Hungary the fascist Jobbik is now the third biggest parliamentary party, with 47 seats. In Sweden the neo-Nazi Swedish Democrats (SD) were elected to parliament for the first time in 2010 gaining 20 seats. In the Netherlands Gert Wilders' racist Party for Freedom (PVV) is now the third largest, with 24 seats. In the US we have seen the dramatic rise of the Tea Party, a loose grouping of right wing Republicans, Christian fundamentalists and racists who are in part using Islamophobia to push the Republican Party further to the right. In this country the British National Party (BNP), while it may be in the process of ripping itself apart, still has two MEPs and remains a major threat. But the biggest danger today is the English Defence League (EDL).

Cameron's Munich speech was delivered on the same day as an EDL march in Luton. Cameron's timing was no accident. The EDL were returning to the town that spawned them and they boasted, wrongly as it turned out, that this was going to be their biggest march ever. Cameron's message was not lost on Stephen Yaxley Lennon, better known as Tommy Robinson, the leader of the EDL. On the Luton demonstration he boasted to his supporters that Cameron was "now saying what we're saying. He knows his base".[1]

For many anti-racists the rise of the EDL, a racist street fighting movement, seemed to emerge from nowhere. The EDL has already spawned the Scottish Defence League (SDL) and the Welsh Defence League (WDL). There are now Defence League type organisations being set up in other countries across Europe. The man pulling the organisation's strings was revealed to be millionaire businessman and fundamentalist Christian Alan Lake. In September 2009 he addressed a conference in Malmo, Sweden, entitled "4 Freedoms Worldwide". The conference, organised by the far-right Swedish Democrats, heard Lake tell delegates that it was necessary to build an anti-jihad movement that was "ready to go out onto the street". He also claimed that he and his friends had already begun to build alliances with football supporters.[2]

One month later Lake told a *Daily Telegraph* journalist, "We are worn out with words—you need to have people on the streets. You have to get the message out." The article went on to claim that Lake was seeking to harness football hooligan "firms" by timing demonstrations to coincide with matches. Lake boasted, "These guys [football hooligans] are prepared to demonstrate, and they are already there because there is a match. This is a dirty, nasty, difficult struggle and you have to work with what is available".[3]

And nasty and dirty work is what the EDL have been doing since their formation over two years ago. The roots of the EDL go back to Luton in March 2009. On that day troops from the Royal Anglian Regiment held a welcome home from Afghanistan parade through the town's streets. An angry crowd set upon a small group of young Muslims protesting at the march-past. In the aftermath of the skirmish a group of football hooligans and fascists organised two anti-Islam protests in Luton on 13 April and 24 May 2009. The May provocation ended with hundreds of thugs rampaging through the town's Asian area.

In an attempt to build on the success of Luton the EDL was launched and organised a protest in Birmingham (8 August 2009). Unite Against Fascism (UAF) organised a counter-protest, thousands turned up and the EDL was run out of town. When the EDL organised a second protest in the city (5 September), the Socialist Workers Party and groups of Asian youths organised a counter-protest and once again the EDL was forced to flee the city. An organisation calling itself "Stop the Islamification of Europe" tried to jump on the EDL bandwagon, calling a protest in Harrow, north west London (11 September 2009). And again thousands of black, white and Asian youth supported UAF's call; they too sent the racist thugs packing.

The EDL was clearly put on the back foot, and many claimed that the racist movement was stillborn. But despite opposition, a series of protests over the next few months enabled EDL leaders to build up their forces. An EDL demonstration in Manchester (10 October 2009) saw 700 EDL members take to the streets opposed by 1,400 on the UAF counter-protest. The WDL then organised marches in Swansea on 18 October 2009 and a week later in Newport, South Wales, and once again they were opposed by large numbers of anti-fascists. On 31 October 2009 about 900 EDL supporters protested in Leeds and were met by 1,500 UAF supporters. Around 500 EDL protesters assembled in Nottingham on 5 December 2009 following an earlier parade by members of the 2nd Battalion, The Mercian Regiment returning from Afghanistan.[4]

From January 2010 to May 2011 there were at least 20 more "official" EDL demonstrations. The numbers joining the EDL protests have fluctuated, so in Stoke (January 2010), Bolton (March 2010), Dudley (April 2010), Bradford (August 2010) between 2,000 and 4,000 marched, but only 200 marched in Cardiff (June 2010) and 150 in Weymouth (April 2011).[5]

The EDL is a very secretive top-down organisation run on military lines. Tommy Robinson and his cousin Kevin Carroll are joint leaders. Below them are a small inner circle of activists. The EDL is organised through a combination of area-based divisions and much smaller "specialist" divisions like their "soldiers" division, "women's" divisions and "Jewish" and "Sikh" divisions. Many in these divisions wear paramilitary outfits and black hoodies with their division group imprinted on them. In the summer of 2010 the divisions were grouped into regions and led by a regional organiser. These were put in place in an attempt to stop the internecine fights that have broken out periodically in the EDL. The leadership had to issue a "code of conduct" that stated, "No member should supersede this chain of command without good reason…division leaders or RO must be obeyed at all times".[6] Clearly no democracy issues here.

The EDL's foot soldiers are drawn from a number of football hooligan "firms". They come from a number of clubs including Chelsea, Queens Park Rangers, Luton, Aston Villa, Wigan, Wolverhampton and Preston North End. The media likes to portray these hooligans as working class yobs. No survey has been conducted on the class base of the EDL. But what little we know about them suggests that their leadership comes from what Karl Marx described as the "petty bourgeoisie"—the classic base of fascism. For example, Tommy Robinson runs his own tanning shop in Luton, Kevin Carroll is a self-employed builder and the spokesperson at the Harrow Stop the Islamification of Europe protest was an American student based at King's College London. Two well-known Chelsea hooligans were identified leading the EDL protest in Stoke. One is employed in the City of London and is known to donate £500 a month to the BNP and the other runs his own van company. And as I have pointed out, Alan Lake, the "brains" behind the EDL, is a millionaire.

This is not a spontaneous movement, as some claim. The fact that many EDL divisions are based around so-called football hooligan firms means they have some social cohesion. Over the last two decades football clubs have been rightly determined to stamp out violence on the terraces. This effort, and increased policing and surveillance at stadiums have forced the violence underground and away from the grounds. This in turn has led to the development of well-organised networks of football gangs, who are able to organise fights in secluded areas, avoiding police detection and infiltration.

The second factor that has aided the Defence Leagues is the internet. Much of their organising has been done through the EDL website and numerous Facebook groups. The EDL claim they now have over 80 branches, many of which meet on a monthly basis to plan activities, "flash protests" and demonstrations.

Although many are drawn to the Defence Leagues by the promise of violence, the political cement that holds them together is anti-Muslim racism. Across Europe we have seen a terrifying rise in Islamophobia. As long ago as 1997 the Runnymede Trust think-tank produced a report on the rise of Islamophobia.[7] Since 9/11 and 7/7 we have seen a sharp increase in racist attacks on Muslims, mosques and Asian shops. Islam has been vilified by large sections of the British media and the political establishment to levels that draw comparison with the anti-Semitism directed at Jewish people in 1930s.

Islamophobia manifests itself in a variety of debates, for example over multiculturalism, and national and international security. The rapid growth in Islamophobia and the moral panics that surround it are an urgent wake-up call for anti-racists. They mark a significant shift in the politics of exclusion, hatred and scapegoating. We are seeing the entwining of a number of related factors; imperialist wars and occupations, the "war on terror" at home (the *Guardian* newspaper has highlighted the fact that Asian people are 42 times more likely than other ethnic groups to be held under the terror laws)[8] and a domestic racist agenda, which blames Muslims for many of society's ills. This virulent and potent mixture is fuelling the rise of the EDL and is giving it political legitimacy.

The rise of the EDL is as rapid as it is shocking—but it can be explained. The EDL are growing in a period of profound economic crisis and their supporters' fears and frustrations are directed at Muslims. Taking to the streets in large numbers with the thrill of street violence gives these young (mainly) men a sense of power and prestige they lack in their everyday lives. This is the perfect breeding ground for fascism, which is why at the heart of the EDL lie the Nazi British National Party and other assorted fascist grouplets.

From its very beginnings members of the BNP have played a central role in building and directing the EDL. For instance Chris Renton, the man who was behind the EDL website, is a BNP member, as is Darren Cooling the administrator of the Luton EDL. One of the organisers of the Birmingham protests was BNP member Richard Price. It has been revealed that Tommy Robinson is an ex-member of the BNP and Kevin Carroll has nominated a BNP election candidate.[9]

Sections of the BNP have seen the EDL as a pool to fish for new recruits to the party. But the reality has proved to be somewhat different, for as the electoral fortunes of the BNP have declined many members have jumped ship and joined the EDL—it has in fact become a bridge out of the BNP. Many rank and file BNP members fed up with electioneering are being attracted to the street thuggery the EDL offers.[10]

The rise of the EDL is not, as some claim, unique in British history. There are clear historical parallels with past anti-Semitic far-right organisations like the British Brothers League and the British Union of Fascists.

The British Brothers League was founded by Captain William Stanley Shaw in 1901, forming a close alliance with Stepney Conservative MP and former colonial Indian Army officer Major William Evans-Gordon. Although the movement was led by Conservative and Liberal MPs its political base lay among the pub landlords of east London. Initially the BBL was not an anti-Semitic organisation; it was more interested in propagandising in favour of east London businesses against cheap foreign imports. But soon its main demands moved away from trade protectionism and it began to scapegoat Russian, Austrian and Polish Jews fleeing oppression migrating to Britain. One of the BBL's main slogans was "England for the English" and anti-Semitism became its motivating force.

The League's first mass meeting took place at the People's Palace, Mile End, in January 1902, with over 4,000 people attending. One local councilor and BBL supporter asked the audience, "Who is corrupting our morals?" He then went on to answer himself with the reply, "The Jews." The call and response session continued: "Who is destroying our Sundays?—The Jews. Who is debasing our national life?—The Jews. Shame on them. Wipe them out."

The crowd poured out of the theatre chanting, "Wipe them out!" Eyewitness reports describe thousand-strong gangs rampaging down East End streets smashing Jewish shops and premises and beating up Jewish passers-by.

The League counted in its ranks 45,000 members (anyone who signed the organisation's manifesto was considered a member). Over the next two years BBL supporters organised menacing parades and attacked migrants and Jews. The Tory government, in order to appease the leaders of the BBL, implemented tariffs on imports and passed the racist Aliens Act of 1905 (the first ever law passed in Britain limiting immigration). The BBL, even after its demise, left its mark in east London. Local fascist A G Plaskett later wrote, "A generation of East Enders were familiarised with a populist movement, basing its tactics on the mass meeting, that allied jingoistic nationalism with anti-alien feeling".[11]

Throughout the 1920s and 1930s Europe saw a rise of fascist movements, including in 1932 the founding of Sir Oswald Mosley's British Union of Fascists (BUF), known as the Blackshirts after their uniform. Three years later the BUF was an openly anti-Semitic organisation concentrating its forces in the east of London, where half of its membership lived. In the course of 1935 and 1936 the BUF held over 2,000 meetings and parades in East London. It put up posters saying "Kill the Jews" and carried out attacks on the Jewish shops and homes. At a rally in Bethnal Green one BUF speaker, Mick Clarke, addressed a 12,000-strong crowd saying it was time the British people knew "that east London's big pogrom is not very far away now". Later that day 200 Blackshirts set fire to cars and smashed and looted Jewish shops. Anyone who looked Jewish was attacked, several Jewish men were razor-slashed and a Jewish hairdresser was thrown through a plate glass window.[12]

This type of fascist street movement developed in other European countries. In Italy in 1919 a group of Benito Mussolini's followers developed a new tactic in rural Northern Italy, "squadrismo". Strong-arm squads, "squadre d'azione", beat up socialists, smashed up printing presses and terrorised anyone who stood in their way. Hitler on his road to power unleashed his "Brownshirts" who attacked socialists, Jews and trade unionists.[13]

The historic parallels are clear. Today we are seeing gangs similar to the EDL gaining momentum across Europe. In Hungary, Jobbik supporters have been involved in a series of assaults on the Roma community.[14] In Russia there has been a sharp rise in attacks on minority communities and once again we are seeing the re-emergence of anti-Semitism and openly fascist organisations.[15]

In describing the rise of fascism in Germany in the 1930s the revolutionary Leon Trotsky wrote, "Fascist movements don't start out as fascist movements, but at the moment this movement begins attacks on the workers, their organisations, their actions and minorities, a fascist movement is born".[16]

The EDL is going through such a political transformation. What began as a proto-fascist movement has become a fully formed fascist/

pogromist organisation. When it was formed it claimed it was a movement only against "militant Islam". That was never true. In reality the EDL is hostile to all Muslims in this country. This became crystal clear when on a demonstration in Preston EDL members chanted "Burn down the mosque".[17] The national EDL launched a petition against the building of any more mosques in April 2011.[18] EDL demonstrations in Stoke, Bradford, Dudley and Luton all ended in mobs of racists trying to attack what they saw as Muslim neighbourhoods.

But it would be a mistake to see the EDL as only an anti-Muslim movement. It is rapidly developing into an organisation with broadening targets, attacking trade union marches, anti-racist meetings, progressive bookshops and socialist gatherings. In May 2010 WDL members attacked a May Day trade union demonstration in Swansea, South Wales.[19] During the student protests in the winter of 2010 Tommy Robinson spoke at an EDL rally in Peterborough, describing students as "dirty, stinking, layabouts" and warned that the EDL would attack student protests.[20] In the first half of 2011 EDL members and a splinter group named the "North West Infidels" launched a series of violent attacks on meetings defending multiculturalism, the most savage taking place in Barking, east London, and Brighton.[21]

However, while the EDL is similar to past fascist movements, it has also adapted to the 21st century. Many, but not all, in the EDL leadership have been prepared to jettison old fascist orthodoxies in order to gain mass appeal. This "modernisation" or "redefining fascism for the 21st century" is not confined to the EDL. Since the end of the Second World War European fascist and far-right parties have struggled to break out from the political margins. The memory of the genocidal Holocaust and popular opposition to Hitler's Nazi regime has meant that any party presenting itself as a descendent of Hitler has been consigned to the fringes. It was the French fascist leader Jean Marie Le Pen who attempted to "modernise" the Front National (FN) in the early 1980s as a way out of the electoral ghetto. He argued that his party had to get rid of its Nazi heritage; its skinhead culture, public worship of past fascist leaders and talk of racial genocide all had to go. Instead he proposed that the FN should present itself as a "respectable" far-right electoral party, ditch the talk of race and concentrate instead on identity politics.

Under Nick Griffin's leadership the BNP has attempted to do the same thing. There are obvious strengths to these new formations, helping parties like the BNP and FN to gain some measure of electoral success. However, the fact remains that behind the public face both organisations retain their core fascist ideological beliefs.

The EDL has gone further. In order to pursue its anti-Muslim agenda and deflect accusations that racism and bigotry are at its core, the league has tried to appeal to members of the Sikh, Jewish and lesbian, gay, bisexual and transgender communities. On EDL demonstrations you will see Star of David and rainbow flags flying alongside the EDL's inflammatory placards. It is a consequence of the very high levels of Islamophobia in British society today that the EDL has even managed to attract a handful of religious zealots and minority groups to its ranks.

The EDL says it supports the state of Israel and even has a "Jewish division", albeit a minuscule group of reactionary ultra right wing Zionists denounced by all major Jewish groups in Britain.[22] In India there are Sikh groups who promote anti-Muslim racism, so it's little surprise then that a handful of British Sikhs align themselves with reactionary forces here. But once again they are a tiny handful of people roundly denounced in their own communities.[23] No one should be fooled—behind the smokescreen the EDL is just like its far-right counterparts.[24]

The EDL's claim that it is not fascist because it supports the "Jewish cause" would be laughable if it wasn't so serious.[25] History shows us that anti-Semitism was not part of the rise of Mussolini fascists in Italy between 1919 and 1922. Mussolini's appeal was his ability to smash the working class and its organisations. Some Jewish people even allied themselves with his programme. It was a terrible miscalculation. After Mussolini's pact with Hitler in 1936 murderous anti-Semitism became a feature of Italian fascism.[26]

Perhaps most worrying for the anti-fascist and anti-racist movement have been the EDL's attempts to organise inside the LGBT community. In Tower Hamlets open EDL supporters tried to organise an East End "Gay Pride rally" in March 2011 after a number of anti-gay stickers were put up in the borough. There was a real danger that Muslims, not homophobia, would have been the focus of people's anger. The EDL supporters who organised the "Pride" were trying to promote the idea that Islam is more reactionary and homophobic than other religions and because Tower Hamlets has a large Muslim population it was more homophobic than other boroughs. Recent surveys have shown that this is just not true.[27] Metropolitan Police figures demonstrate that there is no correlation whatsoever between the size of the Muslim population in any London borough and the level or rise or fall of homophobic attacks.[28] LGBT campaigners, UAF and Love Music Hate Racism activists in Tower Hamlets responded to the EDL threat by putting up posters which read "Say no to homophobia—Say no to Islamophobia". Campaigners ensured that the "Pride" was cancelled (and plans made for a genuine Pride). Lessons have to be learned from this campaign; it is important for anti-racists to build links and unity between the Muslim and LGBT communities and not allow an agenda where one oppressed group is duped into attacking another.

The history, ideology and actions of the EDL that I have outlined signal that anti-racists, anti-fascists and the trade unions must take the rise of the EDL seriously. Tragically some have argued to ignore this movement and refused to support counter-protests against it. This has been a mistake and one which has allowed the EDL to gain a small foothold.

We have to redouble our efforts to defeat the EDL and be clear about what has to be done. Any campaign against the EDL has to be conducted on many different levels. First and foremost there has to be an ideological battle waged against those politicians and sections of the media who are encouraging Islamophobia. It is essential that anti-racists and progressive forces oppose the attacks on multiculturalism and fight to reaffirm and develop an anti-racist culture in our workplaces, schools, colleges and communities. At the same time we should support and encourage those campaigning against the government's policies of austerity, for it is precisely this destruction of working class communities that can create the breeding ground where fascism and racism may flourish.

But we also have to combat the EDL itself. Unite Against Fascism has worked to encourage and lead this struggle. UAF supporters are

Never on our own: Unity matters

working inside the trade union movement, local communities, faith groups and schools and colleges to both warn against the dangers of the EDL and foster a sense of collective opposition to it. UAF produces campaigning materials, its activists speak at meetings nationwide and its sister organisation Love Music Hate Racism organises concerts all over the country.

The EDL is using the football terraces as a base for recruitment. This means anti-fascists have to go to the grounds and take their message to the supporters. By the first half of 2011 UAF campaigners had leafleted over 50 football grounds and spoken at a number of supporter clubs meetings. Supporters at Celtic, Tranmere Rovers, West Ham, Newcastle United, Cambridge United, Cardiff, Stoke and Wimbledon FC have all joined counter-EDL demonstrations or have put on LMHR events.

It is also important that anti-fascists mobilise the biggest numbers possible against the EDL marching. The EDL and its members thrive on the idea that they are "all powerful" and control the streets. Mass protests give our side confidence and deflate and weaken the racists' movement. I previously wrote:

> Anyone who thinks mass protests are outdated should ask those EDL members who tried to march in Birmingham in 2009. UAF and the SWP organised large counter-protests, which drove them out of the city. It created the biggest crisis yet inside the EDL and many supporters talked about throwing in the towel.[29]

The encouraging fact is, that with a few notable exceptions, UAF's counter-demonstrations have been bigger than the EDL. However, with the exception of Birmingham, east London and Harrow, none have had a decisive impact on the day. That means that UAF and other progressive organisations have to campaign to bring about local coalitions of trade unionists, Muslims and anti-racists to combat the EDL's marches of hate.

The rise of the EDL in Britain is part of a wider phenomenon developing at different rates across Europe and there are parallels between it and past racist movements. The EDL has been successful, where others have failed, because it has found new ways of repackaging its vile racist message. This presents the anti-racist-fascist movement with a real challenge. Yes, we must learn from the past but we are also going to have to develop new ways of undermining this new threat. Hopefully this essay and others in this book will play a part in outlining some ways of doing this. Urgency is the key. If we don't act, history is in danger of repeating itself. Now more than ever we need a unified and collective response.

Photo essay:
The EDL

❖❖

KELViN WiLLiAMS

Above: EDL rally "in support of Israel" outside Israeli Embassy, October 2011. Below:
EDL thugs demonstrate against an Islamic Cultural Centre, Dagenham, March 2011

Never on our own: Unity matters

Above: EDL national mobilisation, Blackburn, Lancashire, April 2011
Below: EDL supporter arrested on Remembrance Day 2010.

Kelvin Williams

Unity against bigotry: National demonstration in London against racism, fascism and Islamophobia, November 2010

Never on our own: Unity matters

Kelvin Williams

Never on our own:
the experience of uniting a
community against the EDL

◆◆

DILOWAR KHAN INTERVIEWED BY YURI PRASAD

I came to Britain from Bangladesh in 1976 at the age of nine. At that time east London was a very scary place, something of a racial battleground. Every Sunday the National Front would come to one end of Brick Lane with their skinhead gangs to hold a street meeting, at the end of which they would march together and attack shops and passersby. On one occasion I narrowly avoided a beating because a shopkeeper pulled me inside just as the NF were passing.

The young people in particular lived in fear. We even used to fear going to school because we were in such a small minority. The end of the school day, even in the Church of England primary school I went to, was a particularly tense time. Going home was dangerous and my friends and I were attacked on very many occasions. That situation led to most Bangladeshis deciding to send their children to one particular school so that there would be safety in numbers.

That same feeling has led many immigrant communities to choose to live in the same area; there is a strong feeling that we need security. In 1978 my family lived in a ground-floor flat in Wapping, and every week our windows would be broken. Guy Fawkes Night was always a particularly bad night for us, as we'd get firecrackers put through our letterbox in the middle of the night. It was normal for us to be called "Paki" and to be sworn at in the street.

Trips outside of our immediate neighbourhood were even more dangerous. I remember one occasion, going to buy my school uniform from a shop a few miles away in Poplar and being attacked by a gang of skinheads.

The idea that we Bangladeshis ever chose to live in particular areas because we don't like living near white people is nonsense. The fact is that whenever we moved into an area, like Brick Lane for example, many of the white residents chose to move away because they didn't want to live near us. In particular, they didn't want their children to go to school with us or alongside foreigners in general. Conversely, our parents wanted us to mix with English children. They thought it would help us to improve our language skills and help us to integrate in this country.

Things have improved enormously over the last 30 years. Bangladeshis and other migrant communities have made Tower Hamlets their home and the days of racist gangs stalking children on their way home from school are thankfully behind us. But I worry that in the current climate, where sections of the media and even some politicians are attempting to scapegoat Muslims for many of society's problems, we could stop making progress and start to go backwards.

Something that particularly worries me is the way that today's bigotry is so specifically targeted against Muslims. In the 1970s and 1980s the attacks were directed against Blacks and Asians. In response, we all stood united and fought against them together. Now bigots are deliberately singling out Muslims and hope that they can get support from other immigrant communities. I think that is part of the classic strategy of divide and conquer.

The "war on terror" has accelerated that process and in Britain things changed dramatically after the 7/7 bombings. Despite the fact that almost all Muslims condemned the attacks, we as a community were still blamed by some. In particular, Muslim women who wear the hijab became fearful of going out and even today you might notice that not many use public transport because they fear being treated with suspicion, or being abused and attacked.

One of the tragedies is that until 7/7 very many Muslims were beginning to feel that Britain was their home. One sign of that is that we started to bury our dead here. Until the 1990s many Muslims would send their relatives back to Bangladesh, Pakistan or India to be buried. That practice is not very common today. Another sign is the growing number of purpose-built mosques in Britain. Contrary to what many racists and bigots think, building a mosque is not a sign of wanting to be separate; it is a way of saying, "We belong here. This is our home."

But I get a sense recently that the spirit of united resistance that was there in the 1970s is coming back. People, including many non-Muslims, are saying they that will not leave us to stand alone. You can see that in the way people came together to defend the community, and the East London Mosque in particular, from attack by the English Defence League in the spring of 2010.

People in Tower Hamlets first heard about the EDL after they planned an attack on the Harrow mosque in north west London in September 2009. People helped spread the word of a counter-demonstration by text and many of our young people went to help defend the community in Harrow from attack. When they got there they found that the mosque had worked with many others, including other faith groups and trade unions, and that Muslims were not on their own against the EDL.

So when the EDL threatened us in Tower Hamlets, we decided to use the same model. The EDL, inspired by the documentaries and writings of journalists such as Andrew Gilligan, Martin Bright and others, claimed that Muslims were attempting to turn Tower Hamlets into an Islamic state, which is absolute nonsense. When the Dutch anti-Muslim politician Geert Wilders came to Britain in March 2010, the EDL came to support him and brought placards that read "Close down the East London Mosque". From then we started to hear rumours that they were going to come here to attack us. In June 2010 they singled out an Islamic conference and mounted a campaign calling for it to be banned for having so-called "radical" speakers. This wasn't true, a fact that both the police and the local council confirmed. Despite this, the conference had to be cancelled and this infuriated many young people in particular. They now felt as though everyone was against them.

But one local resident, Glynn Robins, took the initiative and got a campaign to defend the mosque up and running. He sent round a letter saying that the EDL was not welcome in Tower Hamlets and from that a meeting was organised with Unite Against Fascism. A small group of Muslims from the East London Mosque went along and found a large number of non-Muslims there who wanted to join with us to defend the community and we were surprised at how passionate they were about opposing the EDL. We had gone to the meeting having been advised by our elders that the best thing to do was to ignore the racists and their provocations, which they said would go away eventually. This feeling was echoed by the then leadership of Tower Hamlets council.

Nevertheless, we came away from the meeting feeling that we should resist and that we would not be alone if we did.

Something else that convinced me of the need for a counter-demonstration was the knowledge that if we did nothing, the Muslim youth would come out to defend the community regardless, but they would be forced to stand on their own. That would have been a disaster. An organised protest was the best way to channel their anger in a constructive way. We decided a counter-demonstration would be positive, showing that the wider community was united and would not be divided by racism.

At the meeting I proposed that we have a rally at the London Muslim Centre, which is part of the East London Mosque, involving people of all faiths and none so that we could show that we all stood shoulder to shoulder. I wanted our young people to see that the majority white people are not racist or bigoted, that we have many friends and allies among them. The East London Mosque has always been part of the wider community, with many different groups using it as a place to meet. We wanted to continue that tradition.

In the event, the rally was packed. More than 1,000 people came and we couldn't fit everyone in. It really lifted everyone's spirits and proved emphatically that Muslims were not alone. News of the success of the rally spread far and wide, with the Bengali media spreading the word across the country. It also helped defuse some of the tensions between the different youth gangs in the area because people started to see that they had a common enemy in the EDL.

The following week we had our counter-demonstration, even though we knew that the EDL had decided against coming to Tower Hamlets. Around 5,000 people came together for a massive show of unity. Everyone was there. The march was young and old, Bengali, Somali, African-Caribbean and English together with people of all faiths and none.

The EDL threat served to show that we are not alone—it helped to bring us all together. I think that the main reason that the Muslim community in east London resisted pressure not to hold a counter-demonstration is the long history of anti-racism here. In particular, those of us Muslims who were born and brought up in this country believe we have rights and that we have to stand up for them. Britain is our country too.

Don't give an inch:
Why trade unions must
defend multiculturalism

◆◆

BILLY HAYES

It is well understood in the trade unions today that the economic policy of the coalition government is a major assault upon working class living standards. This has rightly led the majority of trade unions to organise in opposition to this policy.

Unfortunately, what is not so well understood is that the social policy of the same government is an equally devastating attack upon the working class. In particular, David Cameron's statements and policies concerning multiculturalism, and the Muslim community and immigrants represents the social corollary of a reactionary economic policy. If you are going to inflict the biggest reduction in living standards since 1945, then a good dose of racism, Islamaphobia and xenophobia helps to divide the opposition.

As usual, the Conservatives demonstrate a degree of intelligence in the manner in which they promote their policy. David Cameron, while steering public opinion towards respectable forms of Islamophobia, also tacks back by insisting that Islam is a good religion, and Muslims are generally peaceful. But it is evident that the suggestion that Muslims have to accept "our" values places them in *total* as a problem for the rest of society.

Of course, these prejudices are not created by a few political speeches. A basic audit of British history would demonstrate that for hundreds of years British policy was premised on the subjugation of large parts of humanity. If you are going to enslave, colonise or super-exploit people and then defining these people as inferior rationalises and justifies the abuse.

Again Cameron displays the confidence that comes from being part of a party and class which was prominent throughout those centuries. He is able to issue an apology on behalf of the government for the murder of Irish people on Bloody Sunday in Derry in 1972. Further, he even lets it drop before journalists that previous British governments were responsible for many of the current problems in the world. Yet the dominant discourse, as outlined in his Munich speech, is to provide aid and comfort to Islamophobia, and a return to narrow British nationalism.

There is a long tradition of institutionalised racism in British society. Naively perhaps, after the murder of Stephen Lawrence and the findings of the Macpherson Inquiry into the failed police investigation, many of us dared to believe that the lesson had been learnt and systematic progress was possible.

But constant vigilance is the custodian of liberty. It has taken the return of the Tory-led coalition government to demonstrate how fragile progress has been in the fight against such racism.

The price to be paid for the promotion of racism, Islamophobia and anti-immigrant prejudices is not just to be measured in the spread of bigotry, attacks on Muslims, and abusive attitudes to immigrant workers. It is also deeply damaging to the economic development of our society.

In a globalised economy, there is a strong bonus for ethnically-diverse nations. Between nations, those who are familiar with the history and makeup of other nations will benefit, being able to address them directly in their own language and offer a kindred face in trade, exchange and negotiations. Multicultural Britain has a competitive advantage in the inter-connected world.

Attempts to suppress, or ignore, the many language and social skills of our population will have the result of isolating our economy from the most dynamics parts of the world economy. The fact is that we have a pool of talent in our population who can directly engage us with markets and market makers in China and India.

The trade unions have a special responsibility to ensure this element of the debate around multiculturalism is not lost. The more open connections to the world economy give the government the potential to address some of our traditional problems of under-investment in the productive economy and over-reliance upon the City of London and the financial sector. All this means new jobs and improved welfare services.

A free movement of people and goods means an introduction of more dynamic forces into our economy. Instead of City short-termism, inward investors will seek long-term commitments if we provide an environment which welcomes the innovation that diversity brings.

Alongside this, immigrants provide a wide variety of advantages especially in the stimulation of domestic economic activity. The economist Philippe Legrain states, in his book *Aftershock*, that immigrants are twice as likely to starts a new business as people born in Britain. A government study found that in 2006 immigration's net contribution to GDP was to add £6 billion to annual growth.

Inward immigration is absolutely necessary. Even the coalition government is forced to recognise this, at the same time as it stokes up popular prejudice against migrants. In a recent article, the former Italian prime minister Massimo D'Alema made the case for net immigration. Today there are 333 million Europeans, but with a present, and still falling, average birth rate this number would shrink to 242 million in the next 40 years. He estimated that 30 million newcomers will be needed if the collapse of EU living standards is to be avoided. He writes, "Immigrants are an asset, not a danger."

It is then most disturbing that there is a growing trend inside the labour movement to also attack multiculturalism. Not only is this damaging to Britain's ethnic minority communities, and a threat to our economic progress, but should this trend dominate the Labour leadership, then it is much less likely that there will be a return of a Labour government in the near future.

The most notable expression of this trend appears to be from the advocates of Blue Labour. In the April 2011 edition of *Progress* magazine, an interview was conducted with Maurice Glasman, who is prominently associated with Blue Labour. "But it is immigration and multiculturalism which has become the big monster that we don't like to talk about." claims Glasman. Mass immigration under Labour, he believes, serves to "act as an unofficial wages policy". The party's position, Glasman contends, occupied a "weird space where we thought that a real assault on the wage levels of English workers was a positive good". He also charges the last government with having acted in a "very supercilious, high handed way: there was no public discussion of immigration and its benefits. There was no election that was fought on that basis. In fact there was a very, very hard rhetoric combined with a very loose policy going on. Labour lied to people about the extent of immigration and the extent of illegal immigration and there has been a massive rupture of trust."

Since Enoch Powell it has been a staple of British political life that politicians will claim to be breaking a taboo by speaking out against immigration. Nothing reveals the lack of innovative thinking more than Glasman invoking this stale cliché.

Further, Glasman is promoting a myth by suggesting that immigration lowers wages. Government research found that a 1 percent increase in the rate of immigrants leads to an increase of up to 0.4 percent in average earnings. The Low Pay Commission found that between 1997 and 2005 immigrants made a positive contribution to the average wage increase experienced by non-immigrant workers.

It takes a wilful myopia to see Glasman as an original political thinker. He continues, "We have essentially devalued our language by making things the opposite of what they mean, and losing "fairness"— which we did at the last election—was actually a catastrophe for us because when we said "fairness" people thought we meant privilege, privilege for the new, privilege for people who don't work, everything calculated on a need and nothing done on desert."

It is certainly a devaluation of language to suggest that unemployment is a "privilege", or that social services are biased towards migrants and asylum seekers. There is no evidence offered for this, because there is none.

Glasman takes his reactionary analysis to a logical point: "Glasman calls on progressives to recognise their 'responsibility for the generation of far right populism', currently manifested in the growth of the English Defence League. 'You consider yourself so opposed that you don't want to talk to them, don't want to engage with them; you don't want anybody with views like that anywhere near the party.' This, he believes, is to ignore 'a massive hate and rage against us' from working class people 'who have always been true to Labour'. The solution, he says, is 'to build a party that brokers a common good, that involves those people who support the EDL within our party. Not dominant in the party, not setting the tone of the party, but just a reconnection with those people that we can represent a better life for them, because that's what they want.' That process begins, argues Glasman, by understanding that 'working class men can't really speak at Labour Party meetings about what causes them grief, concerns about their family, concerns about immigration, love of country, without being falsely stereotyped as sexist, racist/nationalist'."

Glasman obviously isn't above a few stereotypes of his own. He ignores the many white workers who have joined with the black community and participated in the many anti-racist and anti-fascist struggles that have taken place since 1945. Nor does it occur to him just how integrated our multicultural society is. Recent ONS figures show that ethnic minorities now make up nearly one in six of the population of England and Wales. Notably, he has not registered that there is a wide variety of cross-community marriage and families, with over a million people from such mixed marriages. It is much simpler for him to stick with the myth of white, male, working class political impotence.

This is where a rather threadbare and outdated reactionary rhetoric slides into the irresponsible and dangerous. The English Defence League is a violently Islamophobic organisation with a fast growing record of physical attacks, hate speech and racist chants. It is not a radical stance to fail to so identify a pogromist organisation—it is an irresponsible stance.

Further, it is dangerous insofar as it concedes a point where there is only a prejudice. In a *New Statesman* magazine survey published in February 2010, 99 percent of British Muslims were found to believe that attacks in which civilians are the targets are not morally justifiable. 77 percent of Muslims strongly identified with this country; this is despite the fact that Muslims are disadvantaged on about every social measure in British society. The suggestion that EDL supporters are welcome in the Labour Party is a suggestion that Muslims are not.

The defence of multicultural Britain is also a defence of the trade union and labour movement which reflect, often imperfectly and unproportionally, that society.

The BNP is explicit in wanting an all white Britain. The EDL is explicit in wanting to suppress Muslims. It is the duty of the trade unions to explicitly stand up against these organisations, giving not an inch to their racism, Islamophobia, or violent and intimidating activity.

The trade unions must continue to support anti-fascist campaigns and organisations like Unite Against Fascism. It is only through consistent campaigning that we will isolate these new fascists and pogromists. Those politicians who draw them into the wider body of society by attacking multiculturalism are doing a terrible disservice to our society.

Above all, they are unnecessarily gambling with the security of Britain's black communities, ethnic minorities, and particularly Britain's Muslim community. But they are also damaging our economic position, with the inevitable impact upon general living standards.

We must defend multiculturalism—not just because it is phenomenally creative in social, cultural, scientific and artistic terms, but also because it is one of the most powerful forces of production in the globalised economy.

The struggle to build and defend our multicultural society

◆◆

WEYMAN BENNETT

There's a battle of ideas over multiculturalism. That has been clear for some time. But the response of the anti-racist left to this attack has, at times, been muddled. In one respect this isn't a surprise. Multiculturalism has always been contested territory, and its relation to wider issues of racism and inequality is a complex one. But I want to argue that the anti-racist left needs to defend multiculturalism against attacks from the right. And I want to argue that this defence needs to be tied to wider struggles against injustice and against attacks on working people.

Let's start by looking at the history of the concept. Many people think multiculturalism was invented recently. But in fact even in the 1960s and 1970s there was a liberal concept of multiculturalism, in that Britain's rulers recognised immigration from the Commonwealth was necessary, and that this would mean there would be cultural differences within Britain that somehow had a rightful place. But this acceptance came at a price. Black and Asian immigrants could have their own culture, provided it was understood that these were inferior to British culture. In time black people would have to drop their own cultures and merge with the superior British culture. If they didn't, they weren't "really" British.

It's important to understand that Britain's rulers didn't promote this kind of multiculturalism out of the kindness of their hearts. Even hardened imperialists and racists like Enoch Powell paid lip service to it. And that is because it was at heart a concession to the struggles for recognition and independence that erupted across the British Empire after the Second World War. The transformation of the Empire into the Commonwealth, the turn to immigrant labour, and the limited multiculturalism adopted in this period were all double-edged. In part they were about the ruling class taking advantage of a new post-war economic reality and pushing forward a new strategy. In part it was because the struggles of black and Asian people against colonialism and racism had left them with no choice but to do that.

This limited version of multiculturalism lasted until the early 1980s. But the anti-racist movement that grew up in the late 1970s and the 1981 riots forced a new change onto the agenda. Lord Scarman's report after the 1981 Brixton riot talked of African-Caribbean and Asian people suffering from a "cultural deficit". He blamed Brixton and the other riots that year, in part, on the exclusion of black and Asian cultures from official British culture. And he proposed a change in that official culture to overcome that exclusion—in particular, the development of multicultural institutions.

It's important to realise this was break with the old multiculturalism as well as a continuation of it. It was a shift from seeing the diversity of cultures and races in Britain as a problem to be managed to seeing it as a fact of life to be broadly welcomed. The notion that minority cultures could contribute positively to wider culture began gradually to take hold, at least in society at large. This forced the authorities to acknowledge, at least in part and reflected in legislation, that the fundamental problem was racism in society rather than the mere presence of ethnic diversity.

It is this more inclusive and egalitarian version of multiculturalism that is under attack today, by people who want to go back to the days when some kind of "British" or "Western" culture was considered superior. Ironically, many of these people argue against multiculturalism on the grounds that they are defending the Enlightenment project. Yet the Enlightenment was fundamentally based upon freedoms of thought, belief and expression—which today's "enlightened" anti-multiculturalists would seek to withdraw from cultural and religious minorities in Britain.

Their primary target today is Muslims. Anti-Muslim racism has been building for years. We saw New Labour's response to the riots that took place in northern cities a decade ago. It was sharply intensified by the "war on terror" and its associated demonisation of Muslims as somehow being inherently "extremist", "self-segregating" and opposed to "British values". Of course, it's never explained what these "British values" are exactly, or what makes them so uniquely "British". We are told they involve notions of "fair play" and "democracy". The problem with that is even a cursory look at British history shows little regard for such values in practice.

Underlying the current debate over multiculturalism is a fight between racism and anti-racism. And this takes place in a backdrop of economic crisis, with governments across the Western world seeking to implement austerity measures. It is no accident that three leading politicians in Europe—Angela Merkel, Nicolas Sarkozy and David Cameron—have made high profile speeches claiming multiculturalism has "failed" and blaming immigrants for failing to "integrate". They need to promote a myth of national unity—"we're all in it together"—and that in turn involves discovering an "enemy within", or internal "other" that the nation can allegedly unite against.

But the roots of this anti-multiculturalist ideology run deeper. Underlying it is the deeply reactionary idea that social solidarity can only take place between people who are ethnically or culturally similar. *Prospect* magazine editor David Goodhart's 2004 essay entitled "The Discomfort of Strangers" tried to argue that British people only accepted the post-war creation of the welfare state because of the assumption that we all shared common values. He further argued that the lack of a welfare state in the US was a consequence of ethnic diversity—white people did not feel solidarity the black and Hispanic people and did not want a welfare state that would help them. He even appealed to arguments from evolutionary psychology to back up his claim that people always somehow prefer their own kind.

While these arguments are framed in cultural terms, it's not difficult to see how they slip into racial ones. Nobody suggests that the white South Africans or Australians who turn up on our shores somehow undermine the nation's cultural homogeneity. And studies by sociologists such as Charles Zastrow have shown that it is racism, not ethnic diversity as such, that has undermined social solidarity and weakened welfare provision in the US. Where there is collective bargaining it brings black, white and Hispanic workers together, all of them gain benefits and greater healthcare support. Conversely where there is less integration and racism divides the workforce, all workers are worse off. When poor white people identify with rich white people, it is detrimental to their living and health standards. When they identify with other poor people, regardless of colour, culture or creed, they gain economically.

So we need to challenge not just the current attack on multiculturalism, but the whole assumption that the "white working class" is somehow naturally in competition with non-white communities, and that it has values and interests in common that sets it apart from the rest of the working class. We need to assert in contrast that multiculturalism is an essential component of the social unity we need to fight for better public services and a better quality of life. Far from multiculturalism being to blame for the social problems that exist in Britain, it is a vital part of the solution. We need to say clearly that these problems are not caused by the presence of immigrants or by cultural diversity, and that they are everything to do with government policy and the current crisis of capitalism.

There are of course major differences between the sophisticated "cultural" arguments peddled by the likes of Goodhart today and the crude racism of the British Empire based on skin colour and biological hierarchy. The post-war anti-colonial uprisings, the Civil Rights movement and the fall of apartheid have all dealt severe blows to that kind of open and overt racism. But in some respects the new cultural racism is more insidious than its older counterpart. When Enoch Powell made his infamous "Rivers of Blood" speech he was sacked from the Tory shadow cabinet. Margaret Thatcher's comments about Britain being "swamped by people of a different culture" were made before she won the 1979 general election, and she avoided such direct rhetoric when in power. But today we see in David Cameron a Tory prime minister who sees fit to peddle Powellite ideas in major policy speeches. A qualitative line has been crossed when a serving prime minister promotes these notions and builds social policy on them.

The lack of outcry against Cameron's remarks was also worrying. The Labour shadow minister Sadiq Khan spoke out, but very few of his colleagues followed suit. And we saw in Oldham how a Labour MP like Phil Woolas can play the race card against Muslims to attract votes. He has since been stripped of his position, banned from holding office for three years and suspended from the Labour Party. But the incident shows that politicians of all parties are not above using racism as a means of gaining short term political advantage.

We have also seen a dangerous pandering to racist ideas from the "Blue Labour" project being argued by former Blairites and right-wingers inside the party. This posits that immigration is a legitimate reason for white working class discontent, and that an emphasis on "faith, family and flag" can win these white working class voters back. These are exactly the same kind of arguments promoted in France in the early 1980s—and they helped shore up Jean-Marie Le Pen's Front National by blaming immigrants blaming for the decline in employment and housing opportunities.

What all these "Blue Labour" arguments ignore is the extent to which multiculturalism and multiracial struggle have shaped British society and deeply embedded themselves into the country's social and political fabric. Britain has been a multiracial, multicultural society for hundreds of years now. While Britain has an appalling history of racism, it also has an inspiring history of people—black and white—rejecting that racism. As far back as the 18th century the working class movement in this country has campaigned against slavery and involved black leaders and radical activists such as William Cuffay, William Davidson, Olaudah Equiano and Robert Wedderburn. The working class in this country was born into anti-racist and anti-imperial struggle. The Chartists flew the tricolour in solidarity with the Irish struggle. Lancashire cotton workers identified with the Union side of the US Civil War, and rejected arguments from their bosses that their economic interests lay with the Confederacy. When Mahatma Gandhi visited Britain it was the trade union movement, including Lancashire women cotton workers that greeted him and made him welcome.

And that tradition has continued into the present day. Trade unions were at the forefront of the struggle against the National Front in the 1970s and the wider battles against racism in the 1980s. From the mid-1970s onwards you saw trade unions organising black and white workers on a united basis—in contrast with some of the practices from the 1950s and 1960s. It was the National Union of Teachers that first challenged headmaster Ray Honeyford's reactionary views on race in Yorkshire in the 1980s. It was the Trades Union Congress that first gave a platform to the family of murdered black teenager Stephen Lawrence. Today every trade union has an equalities unit and most branches have an equalities officer. Anti-racism is an integral and ineradicable feature of the organised working class.

It is that tradition that offers the best hope of defending our multicultural society and fighting back on all sort of other fronts—against the Tory government's cuts, and against fascist organisations seeking to further whip up race hatred on the ground. As I write this article the British National Party has faced a significant decline in its fortunes, in contrast to the rise of fascist groups or racist populist groups across much of Europe. Why is this? Some claim "British culture" is uniquely anti-fascist, but that claim is difficult to square with the historical reality of the Blackshirt movement in the 1930s, the National Front's initial successes in the 1970s or the BNP's electoral breakthroughs. The real explanation is the power and willingness of the organised working class in Britain to combat racism and fascism. Millions of workers are still organised into trade unions and these unions are able to disseminate information and political arguments that counter the barrage of racist propaganda in the mass media. Trade unions have played a vital role in arguing for unity against fascist forces don't just whip up racism, sexism and homophobia but also aim to smash the trade union movement or any other organisation that seeks to defend the working class.

We've seen that power exercised in recent history with the very determined trade union involvement in campaigns against the Nazis whenever they've presented themselves. The destruction of the National Front was a consequence of both the formation of the Anti Nazi League and the wider anti-racist struggles of the time led by militant black and Asian youth and workers. The Anti Nazi League initiated a tradition of unity against the fascists that brought together Labour Party activists such as Peter Hain with revolutionary left organisations such as the Socialist Workers Party. This unity was instrumental in creating a united front that could mobilise hundreds and thousands of people against the National Front, whether through direct demonstrations against them or through mass propaganda through campaigns such as Rock Against Racism. This helped win people's hearts and minds to a new anti-racist sensibility that profoundly changed the nature of Britain and played a huge positive role in the lives of black and Asian people here. By the 1980s racism was no longer respectable. It was something that was opposed in trade unions, in workplaces and in schools. I witnessed this myself growing up in east London in the 1970s in an atmosphere poisoned by the National Front, and seeing this situation transformed over the following decade as people of all backgrounds came together to oppose the NF and campaign against racism.

It is that tradition of united, militant and principled campaigning that has dealt body blows to the BNP in Barking & Dagenham and Stoke-on-Trent, where Unite Against Fascism and its sister platform Love Music Hate Racism has worked in conjunction with local anti-fascist campaigners, trade unionists and Labour Party activists to successfully drive the Nazis out of the council chamber. In contrast, where politicians have pandered to racist ideas or made concessions to the far right, these fascist organisations have ultimately gained in strength and influence. You only have to look to France, where Sarkozy's deportation of Roma and anti-Muslim rhetoric has pushed Marine Le Pen high up in the opinion polls. We have seen an ugly escalation in attacks on Muslim and Roma elsewhere in Europe, again showing the dangers of what happens when mainstream politicians give the fascists credence by blaming minorities for causing crime and social deprivation.

The attacks on multiculturalism are coming from people who want to turn the clock back to the 1950s and revive the myth of authentically "British" culture as superior to and opposed to the culture of an internal "other". The minority cast in that role keeps changing—it used to be the Irish, then it was the Jews. Today it is Muslims.

We need a struggle on two fronts. Firstly, we have to fight the hard racist ideas of fascist movements like the BNP and the English Defence League. That means stopping them from marching through our city centres terrorising Muslims and attacking mosques. It also means stopping the Nazis at the ballot box when they try to win council seats.

We also need to fight on a second front against the softer and more sophisticated racist ideas peddled by journalists and politicians. We need to combine militant anti-fascist activity on the ground with a principled anti-racist defence of the multicultural society we have fought so hard to create. We have every reason to think we can win that fight.

NOTES

SECTION ONE
Reaching for racism: That speech in Munich

Ken Livingstone:
In praise of multicultural London

1   http://www.progressives.org.uk/articles/article.asp?a=7981
2   http://www.fearandhope.org.uk/project-report/
3   http://www.greenbergresearch.com/index.php?ID=2445

Liz Fekete:
Understanding the European-wide assault on multiculturalism

1   For a discussion of those arguments, and how they were revived during the premiership of Margaret Thatcher, see Nancy Murray, 'The press and ideology in Thatcher's Britain', *Race & Class*, winter 1986.
2   Interview with Torbjørn Røe Isaksen, *Klassekampen*, 15 February 2011. Translation by Mari Linløkken.
3   *Austrian Independent*, 7 October 2010.
4   *Austrian Independent*, 4 October 2010.
5   See the critique of Carla Anna Baghajati, "Almost worse than Strache", *Die Presse*, 4 November 2009.
6   *Guardian*, 18 October 2010.
7   *Guardian*, 18 October 2010.
8   *Migration News Sheet*, December 2010.
9   DutchNews.nl, 15 February 2011.
10   Agence France Presse, 12 February 2011.
11   Pind resigned as a member of the board in 2009 following the prosecution of its chair, Lars Hedegaard—a member of the anti-immigrant Danish People's Party—who was acquitted on a technicality of violating Danish anti-racism laws following a prosecution for comments to the effect that girls in Muslim families are "raped by their uncles, their cousins or their fathers". Free Press Society-Denmark was created in 2004 by Lars Hedegaard, a newspaper columnist, citing increasing pressure on free speech, and the "cartoons crisis". It is linked to the International Free Press Society whose Board of Advisors includes leading neoconservatives and New Right figures such as Daniel Pipes, Robert Spencer, Geert Wilders and regular Fox News commentator Andrew Bostom.
12   *Copenhagen Post*, 9 and 17 March 2011.
13   Cameron's speech on radicalisation and Islamic extremism, Munich, 5 February 2011, www.newstatesman.com/blogs/the-staggers/2011/02/terrorism-islam-ideology
14   Speech delivered on 20 April 1968 which continued, "As I look ahead, I am filled with foreboding. Like the Roman I seem to see 'the River Tiber foaming with much blood'."

15 "Quand les assises de l'Islamisation applaudissent Michel Onfray", *Les Indigènes de la République*, 16 January 2011.

16 *EU Observer*, 16 October 2010.

17 The accusation was made by Claudia Roth, the co-chair of the Green Party. See *Guardian*, 11 October 2010.

18 *Guardian*, 4 March 2011.

19 Jürgen Habermas, "Leadership and Leitkultur", *New York Times*, 28 October 2010.

20 *Migration News Sheet*, November 2010.

21 *Migration News Sheet*, November 2010.

22 The junior partner in the coalition government seems to be hostile to the stance taken by the other two parties, which seems driven by the Christian Social Union, which has strong roots in Bavarian Catholicism. Justice minister Sabine Leutheusser-Schnarrenberger (Free Democrat Party, FDP) attacked the minister, stating, "Of course Islam belongs in Germany", adding that, "I assume that the new minister will follow the lead of his predecessor and will take his responsibility for integration policy seriously, and campaign for cohesion rather than exclusion"—*Guardian*, 4 March 2011.

23 Deutsche Presse Agentur, 2 November 2010.

24 http://www.stern.de/tv/sterntv/stern-tv-debatte-zur-integration-deutschenfeindlichkeit-realitaet-an-schulen-1615218.html

25 *Migazin*, 24 March 2011.

26 *Earth Times*, 7 November 2010.

27 As cited in *Guardian*, 11 February 2011.

28 *Telegraph*, 12 December 2010.

29 *Financial Times*, 9 February 2011.

30 *Guardian*, 17 October 2010.

31 *Der Spiegel*, 15 July 2010.

32 · *Dutch News*, 2 November 2010.

33 *Guardian*, 14 April 2010.

34 *Migration News Sheet*, November 2010.

35 *Copenhagen Post*, 7 April 2011.

36 Associated Press, 6 March 2011.

37 *Guardian*, 18 March 2011.

38 *Deutsche Welle*, 9 November 2010.

Tariq Modood:
Multiculturalism and integration: struggling with confusions

1 This chapter is based on my contribution to the British Academy "New Paradigms in Public Policy" project. I would like to thank my colleagues in the project, especially its chair, Peter Taylor-Gooby, and two anonymous referees for their comments; and also Bhikhu Parekh, Geoff Levey, Nasar Meer, Varun Uberoi and Aleksandra Lewicki. For the longer piece, see N Meer and T Modood, "How does Interculturalism contrast with Multiculturalism?", *Journal of Intercultural Studies* (forthcoming).

2   The concern here is not primarily in relation to socio-economic integration, for which see Loury, Modood and Teles (2005) and Heath and Cheung (2007). The bigger challenge—for another occasion—is to connect the socio-economic with the issues discussed in this chapter. I would insist, however, the issues of "difference" are as important as the socio-economic in relation to equal citizenship and have to be understood in their own terms.

3   I do not here mean that there should be a world government or primarily even the ethical view that one should be a citizen of the world, I am here characterising a mode of integration within a country that emphasises a mixing of people from all over the world as in the expression "London is a cosmopolitan city". British sociologists sometimes use the term "multiculture" but this clearly has not carried over into public discourse. It has been suggested to me that the term "interculturalism" best fits here but in the place where it is most used in relation to national politics, Quebec, it is closer to what here I call "individualist-integration". More generally, it is not clear that "interculturalism" includes anything that is not or cannot be included in multiculturalism (see Meer and Modood, forthcoming). I did also consider the term "diversity" but it's either too descriptive and generic and does not pick out a mode of integration or has been appropriated as "diversity management" by human resource professionals.

4   This is how the term has been used by the leading political theorists such as Taylor (1994), Kymlicka (1995) and Parekh (2000) and by the Canadian government; and is consistent with CMEB (2000) and other exponents of multiculturalism—see Modood, 2007: 14-20 for details.

5   British exponents of this view tend, however, to put some communal identities in a normative, privileged position. This particularly applies to political blackness and to some extent to non-cultural political identities generally (Modood 1994).

6   Hence the irony that anti-multiculturalists like President Sarkozy are trying to create corporate representations for Muslims in France; while pro-diversity authors call for the cessation of government meetings with Muslim community leaders (Sen 2006; Malik 2011).

References

Appiah, K A (1994), "Identity, Autenticity, Survival: Multicultural Societies and Social Reproduction", in *Multiculturalism, Examining The Politics of Recognition*, edited by A Gutmann, Princeton University Press: 149-164.

Barry, B (2001), *Culture and Equality: An Egalitarian Critique of Multiculturalism*, Polity.

Brett, J, and A Moran (2011), "Cosmopolitan Nationalism: Ordinary People Making Sense of Diversity", *Nations and Nationalism* 17(1): pp188-206.

Cantle, T (2001), *Community Cohesion: A Report of the Independent Review Team*, Home Office London.

CMEB (2000), *The Future of Multi-Ethnic Britain: Report of the Commission the Future of Multi-Ethnic Britain*, Runnymede Trust.

Fenton, S, and R Mann (2011), "'Our Own People': Ethnic Majority Orientations to Nation and Country", in *Global Migration, Ethnicity and Britishness*, edited by T

Modood and J Salt, Palgrave.

Gallup (2009), The Gallup Coexist Project: Muslim West Facts Project. Available at http://www.euro-islam.info/wp-content/uploads/pdfs/gallup_coexist_2009_ interfaith_relations_uk_france_germany.pdf (accessed on 28 March 2011).

Gilroy, P (2000), *Between Camps: Nations, Culture and the Allure of Race*, Allen Lane.

Hall, S (1998), "Aspiration and Attitude... Reflections on Black Britain in the Nineties", *New Formations* 33 (Spring): 38-46.

Heath, A, and J Roberts (2008), "British Identity: Its Sources and Possible Implications for Civic Attitudes and Behaviour", available at http://www.justice. gov.uk/docs/british-identity.pdf (accessed on 28 March 2011).

Heath, A F, and S Y Cheung (2007), *Unequal Chances: Ethnic Minorities in Western Labour Markets*, published for The British Academy by Oxford University Press.

Jenkins, R (1967), 'Racial Equality in Britain' in *Essays and Speeches by Roy Jenkins*, edited by A Lester, Collins.

Kymlicka, W (1995), *Multicultural Citizenship*, Oxford University Press.

Loury, G C, T Modood and S M Teles, eds (2005), *Ethnicity, Social Mobility and Public Policy: Comparing the USA and UK*, Cambridge University Press.

Malik, K (2011), "I Am Still A Critic of Multiculturalism, Honest", Pandemonium http://kenanmalik.wordpress.com/2011/02/10/still-a-critic-of-multiculturalism/ (accessed 30 March 2011).

Meer, N, and T Modood (2009), "The Multicultural State We're In: 'Multiculture' and the Civic Re-balancing' of British Multiculturalism", *Political Studies* 57 (3), pp473-497.

Modood, T (1994), "Political blackness and British Asians", *Sociology* 28(4): 859-876.

Modood, T (1998), "Anti-Essentialism, Multiculturalism and the 'Recognition' of Religious Minorities", *Journal of Political Philosophy* 6(4): 378-399.

Modood, T (2007), *Multiculturalism: A Civic Idea*, Polity.

Modood, T, and J Dobbernack (2011), "A Left Communitarianism? What about Multiculturalism?", *Soundings*.

Mouritsen, P (2008), "Political Responses to Cultural Conflict: Reflections on the Ambiguities of the Civic Turn" in P Mouritsen and K E Jørgensen, eds, *Constituting Communities: Political Solutions to Cultural Conflict*, Palgrave: pp1-30.

Parekh, B C (2000), *Rethinking Multiculturalism: Cultural Diversity and Political Theory*, Harvard University Press.

Pew Research Center (2006), *The Great Divide: How Westerners and Muslims View Each Other*, available at http://pewglobal.org/2006/06/22/the-great-divide-how-westerners-and-muslims-view-each-other (accessed on 28 March 2011).

Sen, A (2006), *Identity and Violence*, Allen Lane.

Taylor, C (1994), "The politics of recognition" in *Multiculturalism and 'The politics of Recognition': An Essay*, edited by A Gutmann, Princeton University Press: 25-73.

Vertovec, S (2007), "Super-diversity and its Implications", *Ethnic and Racial Studies* 30(6): 1024-1054.

Waldron, J (1991), "Minority cultures and the cosmopolitan alternative", *University of Michigan Journal of Law Reform* 25: 751.

Weldon, F (1989), *Sacred Cows*, Chatto & Windus.

Sabby Dhalu:
One Society Many Cultures

1   http://www.bbc.co.uk/news/10611398
2   http://news.bbc.co.uk/1/hi/world/europe/8652861.stm
3   http://www.bbc.co.uk/news/10316696
4   http://today.yougov.co.uk/life/burqa-ban
5   http://www.inspiredbymuhammad.com/
6   ttp://eifoundation.net/faq.html
7   http://www.channel4.com/news/media/pdfs/Muslims_under_siege_LR.pdf
8   http://centres.exeter.ac.uk/emrc/publications/Islamophobia_and_Anti-Muslim_
    Hate_Crime.pdf
9   http://badmatthew.blogspot.com/2005/09/danny-dorling-replies-to-trevor.html
10 http://www.ccsr.ac.uk/staff/Ludi/documents/UrbS_41_3_2004.pdf
11 http://www.humanities.manchester.ac.uk/socialchange/publications/working/
    documents/CeriPeach-Newsegregation8.pdf
12 http://www.onesocietymanycultures.org/

Danny Dorling:
Multicultural Britain—that's just the way it is

1   As quoted by Sabby Dhalu in 2011 in her text, "Celebrate and defend our
    multicultural society: a response to the *Searchlight* 'Fear and Hope' report",
    March 2011. The full text can be found at http://uaf.org.uk/2011/03/
    a-response-to-the-searchlight-fear-and-hope-report/
2   Michael Pugh, "Drowning not Waving: Boat People and the Humanitarianism at
    Sea", *Journal of Refugee Studies*, 17: 1 (2004) pp50-69 (quote from page 52).
3   The league existed from 1902 until 1923 was in effect, superseded by the British
    Union of Fascists. It had Conservative MPs amongst its membership and was
    held largely responsible for the 1905 Aliens Act being implemented by parliament.
    http://en.wikipedia.org/wiki/British_Brothers_League

Zita Holbourne:
Multiculturalism

1   © Zita Holbourne 2011

SECTION TWO
Horrible histories: Myths of tolerance and nationhood

Edie Friedman:
A place of refuge? Scapegoating "the other"—the treatment of Jewish refugees

1   *Manchester City News*, 12 May 1888.
2   Roy Greenslade, "Seeking Scapegoats—the coverage of asylum in the UK press"

(IPPR, 2005): "…but also important differences: the tone has become more hysterical, the repetitious nature of the stories is more prevalent, and the power of newspapers to set the agenda—both for other media and within the political arena—is more potent, in spite of their declining sales."

3 Pogrom usually refers to an officially sanctioned, organised massacre of Jews, primarily in Russia.

4 Robert Winder, *Bloody Foreigners: the Story of Immigration to Britain* (Little, Brown, 2004), p197.

5 Tony Kushner and Katherine Knox, *Refugees in an Age of Genocide* (Frank Cass, 1999), p25.

6 One of the champions of the aliens' cause was the then young Winston Churchill who in 1904 in a letter to *The Times* stated that there was no good reason for Britain to give up "the old tolerant and generous practice of free entry and asylum to which this country has so long adhered and from which it has so greatly gained". Quoted in Winder.

7 Anne Karpf, *The War After* (Minerva, 1996), p174.

8 As quoted by Winder, p178.

9 Kushner and Knox, p74. Jews were not the only group who were the subject of the prevailing anti-alien sentiment. The Chinese community and, of course, the German community were also targeted.

10 Kushner and Knox, p9. Britain, similar to other western European countries such as France, Netherlands and Belgium, was determined to offer primarily temporary, not permanent, refuge. This is in contrast to the US which, though it also took a paltry number of refugees, saw itself as a country of "permanent integration".

11 *Sunday Express*, June 1938.

12 Karpf, p178.

13 A J Sherman, *Island Refuge: Britain and the Refugees from the Third Reich* (Elek Books, 1973), p48.

14 Louise London, *Whitehall and the Jews 1933-1948, British Immigration Policy and the Holocaust* (Cambridge University Press, 2000), p278.

15 London, p277.

16 London, p12. At the start of the Second World War there were over 78,000 refugees in the UK, of whom some 70,000 were Jewish (excluding accompanied children). The number of Jews who were not allowed to come to Britain was ten times that.

17 Kushner and Knox, p157.

18 Mixed attitudes to new immigrants are not uncommon among established immigrants. A YouGov survey for the Commission for Racial Equality (June 2004) found that of the non-white people interviewed, 35 percent had either a fairly low or very low opinion of people seeking asylum in Britain today (http://www.yougov.com/archives/pdf/RCF040101001_1.pdf). Other research which highlights this ambivalence is found in the IPPR 2005 Survey.

19 Karpf, p185.

20 Karpf, p2.

21 Ironically, post-war Britain (like the US) became a haven for Nazi collaborators and war criminals. David Cesarani, *Justice Delayed* (Mandarin, 1992), quoted in Karpf.

22 London, p12.

23 London, p198. Between the period 1945-1950, 200,000 refugees, immigrant workers and Displaced Persons were admitted to Britain. Only around 1,200 were Jews, whereas over 10,000 Latvians were admitted.

24 London, p282.

25 London, p15.

26 London, p15.

27 Graham D Macklin, "A quite natural and modern defensive feeling? The 1945 Hampstead 'anti-alien' petition" in *Patterns of Prejudice*, Vol 37, No 3 (September 2003), p298.

28 Macklin, p299.

29 This theme was prominent in speeches made by the then Conservative leader, Michael Howard during the 2005 general election campaign.

30 Tony Kushner, "Meaning nothing but good: ethics, history and asylum-seeker phobia in Britain" in *Patterns of Prejudice*, Vol 37, No 3 (September 2003), p266.

31 Kushner, p267.

32 *Daily Express*, 15 May 2002.

33 Quoted in *The Listener*, 16 September 1982, or Max Hastings in *The Guardian*, 11 March 2004.

34 Macklin, p287.

35 Karpf, pp173-5.

36 Yasmin Alibhai-Brown, *Who Do We Think We Are? Imagining the New Britain* (Allen Lane, The Penguin Press, 2000), Introduction, p7.

37 Alibhai-Brown, p92.

38 The Medical Foundation for the Care of Victims of Torture was established 25 years ago under the auspices of the Medical Group of Amnesty International. It aims to provide survivors of torture in the UK with medical treatment, practical assistance and psychotherapeutic support, document evidence of torture, provide training for health professionals working with torture survivors, educate the public and decision-makers about torture and its consequences and ensure that Britain honours its international obligations towards survivors of torture, asylum seekers and refugees.

39 Kushner and Knox, p399.

Gary McFarlane: Ruling Britannia: Capitalism, class and culture

1 Terry Eagleton, "Culture and Barbarism: metaphysics in a time of terrorism", *Commonweal*, March 2009.

2 Raymond Williams, *Culture and Society 1780-1950* (Penguin, 1971).

3 Eagleton.

Hassan Mahamdallie:
Part of their class: Muslim working class struggles in Britain

1 For more on my analysis of Muslims and the war on terror see "Racism: Myths and Realities", *International Socialism* 95 (summer 2002); "Racism", in Farah

Reza (ed), *Anti Imperialism: A Guide for the Movement* (Bookmarks, 2003); and "Racism: A Boost for the Bigots", *Socialist Review*, November 2005, http://www.socialistreview.org.uk/article.php?articlenumber=9579

2   For good accounts of this early history see Humayun Ansari, *The Infidel Within: Muslims in Britain since 1800* (Hurst & Company, 2004), and Nabil Matar, *Turks, Moors and Englishmen in the Age of Discovery* (Columbia University Press, 1999).

3   In the east London docks in the early 1940s there were still Somali and Bangladeshi cafes open along Cable Street, giving rise to speculation that Muslim seamen may have taken part in the 1936 Battle of Cable Street against Mosley's fascists.

4   Richard I Lawless, *From Ta'izz to Tyneside: An Arab Community in the North East of England During the Early 20th Century* (University of Exeter Press, 1995), p220.

5   See Ansari, as above, pp60, 61.

6   See Rozina Visram, *Asians in Britain: 400 Years of History* (Pluto Press, 2002).

7   Havelock Wilson started off as a militant fighter, a working activist like Tom Mann, but moved to the right and by the end of the First World War was getting secret payments from an anti-Labour pro-empire organisation.

8   Lawless, as above, p92.

9   Peter Fryer, *Staying Power: The History of Black People in Britain* (Pluto Press, 1984), p307.

10   Neil Evans, "Regulating the Reserve Army: Arabs, Blacks and the Local State in Cardiff, 1919-45", in Kenneth Lunn (ed), *Race and Labour in 20th Century Britain* (Frank Cass, 1985), p73.

11   Fryer, as above, p300.

12   As above.

13   Visram, as above, p204.

14   Evans, as above, p80.

15   Evans, as above, p102.

16   Visram, as above, p236.

17   As above, pp267-8.

18   As above, p269.

19   As above, p271.

20   Ansari, as above, p151.

21   Dilip Hiro, *Black British, White British: A History of Race Relations in Britain* (Grafton, 1991), p140.

22   As above, pp139-140.

23   As above, p20.

24   As above, pp269-270.

25   Kim Gordon, *Black Nationalism and Socialism* (SWP, 1979), p69.

26   Jack Dromey and Graham Taylor, *Grunwick: The Workers' Story* (Lawrence and Wishart, 1978), p102.

27   As above, p103.

28   As Ramamurthy records, "Among the founding members of the Bradford Asian Youth Movement were young Asians who had left the International Socialists (IS, forerunner of the Socialist Workers Party, *Militant* and the Revolutionary

Communist Group)"—Anandi Ramamurthy, "The Politics of Britain's Asian Youth Movements", *Race & Class* (Institute of Race Relations), vol 48, 2006, p43.

29 Ramamurthy, as above, p44 (see also the Tandana-Glowworm digitalised archive of Asian Youth Movement political ephemera at www.tandana.org).

30 Ramamurthy, as above, p44.

31 As above, p53.

32 See "Reflecting on the Trial of the Decade: The Bradford Twelve", in *Race Today* vol 14, no 4 (August/September 1982), pp124-132. The two leading members of the group on trial were Gata Aura, who had previously been prominent in the successful fight of Rochdale Pakistani Anwar Ditta to overcome the immigration laws that were preventing her children joining her in Britain, and Tariq Mehmood Ali. Both had been members of the International Socialists. Tariq Mehmood is today a novelist and co-director of the award-winning film *Injustice*—a documentary exposing black deaths in custody. Another defendant was Marsha Singh, who is now a local Labour MP. Lawyers involved in the defence included Helena Kennedy (now a Labour peer) and Ruth Bundy (involved in the Stephen Lawrence inquiry).

33 The contrast between the successful Bradford 12 campaign and its outcome and the trials and "exemplary" sentences handed down following the similar circumstances in Bradford in 2001 is painfully obvious.

34 Ramamurthy, as above, p46.

35 Tariq Mehmood, email conversation with the author, 13 November 2006.

SECTION THREE
Never on our own: Unity matters

Salma Yaqoob:
Muslims, multiculturalism and the politics of dissent

1 "Clegg breaks with Cameron on multiculturalism", *New Statesman*, 3 March 2011.

2 Jenny Bourne, "Germany has failed multiculturalism not vice versa", *Institute of Race Relations*, 21 October 2010.

3 "Cameron's ESOL cuts will make integration harder", *Left Foot Forward*, http://www.leftfootforward.org/2011/04/david-cameron-immigration-speech-esol/

4 Salma Yaqoob, "Did David Cameron really mean what he said about multiculturalism?", *Guardian*, 7 February 2011.

5 Andy McSmith, "Former MI5 chief demolishes Blair's defence of the Iraq war", *Independent*, 21 July 2010.

6 Danny Dorling, "Why Trevor is wrong about race ghettos", *Observer*, 25 September 2005.

7 Maleiha Malik, "Muslims are now getting the same treatment Jews had a century ago", *Guardian*, 2 February 2007.

8 David Batty, "Lady Warsi claims Islamophobia is now socially acceptable in Britain", *Guardian*, 20 January 2011.

9 Peter Oborne, "The shameful Islamophobia at the heart of Britain's press",

Independent, 7 July 2008.

10 "Mail gives more free publicity to irrelevant nutter", *Islamaphobia Watch*, 24 May 2011, http://www.islamophobia-watch.com/islamophobia-watch/2011/5/24/mail-gives-more-free-publicity-to-irrelevantnutter.html

11 "Birmingham Muslims against extremism", 9 February 2011, http://www.salmayaqoob.com/2011/02/birmingham-muslims-against-extremism.html

12 "Mullaney sinks into the sewer", 7 February 2011, http://www.salmayaqoob.com/2011/02/mullaney-sinks-into-sewer.html

13 Salma Yaqoob, "Them and us", *Guardian*, 4 July 2007.

14 Salma Yaqoob, "Muslim women and war on terror", *Feminist Review*, vol 88, issue 1, April 2008.

15 Salma Yaqoob, "Muslims need to take part", Guardian, 21 December 2006.

16 "A victory for equal rights", 19 January 2011, http://www.salmayaqoob.com/2011/01/victory-for-equal-rights.html

17 "£86million scheme to prevent Muslim radicalisation is 'gravy train' for local groups", *Telegraph*, 24 October 2008.

18 Hamed Chapman, "Spy cameras finally removed in Birmingham", *Muslim News*, 27 May 2011 http://www.muslimnews.co.uk/paper/index.php?article=5245

19 http://www.mcb.org.uk/comm_details.php?heading_id=121&com_id=2#jackson

20 Salma Yaqoob, "Did David Cameron really mean what he said about multiculturalism?", *Guardian*, 7 February 2011.

21 Alan Travis, "Officials think UK's Muslim population has risen to 2m", Guardian, 8 April 2008.

22 Inyat Bunglawala, "Honour our Muslim soldiers", *Guardian*, 5 November 2009.

23 "3 out of 4 British Muslims strongly relate to UK", *Link Muslims*, 9 May 2009, http://www.linkmuslims.com/3-out-of-4-british-muslims-strongly-relate-to-uk

24 "Muslim youths in UK feel much more integrated than their European counterparts", *Daily Mail*, 20 August 2009.

25 "TUC and MCB join together to combat Islamophobia and far right threat", TUC Press Release, 5 April 2007, https://www.tuc.org.uk/economy/tuc-13173-fo.cfm

26 "Multiculturalism strengthens communities", *Asian Image*, 28 March 2011, http://www.asianimage.co.uk/news/8936209. Multiculturalism_strengthens_communities/

27 "Sikh community issues ultimatum to EDL's Guramit Singh", *Islamaphobia Watch*, 30 March 2011, http://www.islamophobia-watch.com/islamophobia-watch/2011/3/30/sikh-community-issues-ultimatum-to-edlsguramit-singh.html

**Martin Smith: The English Defence League:
The organ grinders' monkey**

1 http://lancasteruaf.blogspot.com/2011/02/faltering-light-of-little-england.html

2 Martin Smith, *The EDL Unmasked* (*Socialist Review*, 2010), p2. Footage of Lake's speech has now been taken down from the websites but there are a number of blogs and reports verifying the quotes I have attributed to him.

3 http://www.telegraph.co.uk/news/6284184/The-English-Defence-League-will-the-flames-of-hatred-spread.html

4 Smith, as above, p4.

5 http://faith-matters.org/images/stories/fm-reports/english-defense-league-report.pdf.

6 http://www.englishdefenceleague.org/index.php?option=com_content&view=article&id=235:statement-from-tommy-robinson-24th-july&ctid=42:feature-stories

7 *Islamophobia: A challenge for us all, Report of the Runnymede Trust Commission on British Muslims and Islamophobia* (Runnymede Trust, 1997).

8 http://m.guardian.co.uk/uk/2011/may/23/counter-terror-stop-searches-minorities?cat=uk&type=article

9 For examples of BNP members' involvement in the EDL there are numerous articles in the mainstream press exposing those links. For example http://faith-matters.org/images/stories/fm-reports/english-defense-league-report.pdf / http://www.socialistworker.co.uk/art.php?id=20552 / http://uaf.org.uk/2011/02/barnsley-antifascists-march-as-edls-links-to-bnp-exposed

10 The BNP is in the process of tearing itself up at the moment, there have been a number of expulsions and defections. Many branches appear to have shut up shop and joined the EDL.

11 Plaskett played a prominent role in the Bethnal Green branch of Mosley's British Union of Fascists

12 Phil Piratin, *Our Flag Stays Red* (London, 1948).

13 If you want to find out more about the development of fascist gangs in Italy there are two important studies: Paul Corner, *Fascism in Ferrara 1915-1925* (Oxford, 1975), and my dear late friend Tom Behan's brilliant book *The Resistible Rise of Benito Mussolini* (Bookmarks, 2003).

14 Amnesty International have been reporting on Jobbik supporters attacks on the Roma community: http://www.amnesty.org.uk/content.asp?CategoryID=11899

15 I was in Moscow during the riots and saw for myself the violent attacks on non Russian workers. A decent report of events can be found at http://www.guardian.co.uk/world/2010/dec/13/two-dead-football-racist-riot-moscow

16 Leon Trotsky, *Fascism: What It Is and How to Fight It* (Pathfinder, 1993).

17 http://manchesteruaf.org/reports-of-recent-events/107-edl-chanting-qburn-a-mosqueq-in-preston.html

18 http://www.youtube.com/watch?v=Zi7ZpzIXCtU

19 http://uaf.org.uk/2011/03/edl-suspects-in-court-after-alleged-attack=at-socialistmeeting/

20 http://www.youtube.com/watch?v=58RqnpJRm_k&feature=related

21 The attack on the Barking meeting was reported in the local *Barking and Dagenham Post*: http://www.bdpost.co.uk/news/hooded_thugs_attack_office_before_meeting_in_barking_1_903835 and a feature highlighting the wider aspects of recent EDL attacks was reported in the *Guardian* a few days later: http://www.guardian.co.uk/uk/2011/may/27/far-right-attacks-rise

22 http://www.thejc.com/news/uk-news/32535/edl-step-their-jewish-recruitment

23 http://uaf.org.uk/2011/01/sikhs-and-hindus-unite-against-racist-english

-defence-league/

24 Nobody should be confused about the EDL's opportunist support for Jewish/
    LGBT rights; one quick glance at this racist notice board should dispel any such
    doubts: http://northeastpatriot.com/forum/viewtopic.php?f=15&t=90

25 One EDL appeal for new members said anyone can join unless you are a Nazi or
    anti-Semitic.

26 http://www.amazon.co.uk/Benevolence-Betrayal-Italian-Families-Fascism/dp/
    0099223414/ref=sr_1_fkmr0_1?ie=UTF8&qid=1306673062&sr=8-1-fkmr0

27 http://news.pinkpaper.com/NewsStory/5407/24/05/2011/hate-crimes-in-londons-
    soho-on-the-rise-police-say.aspx

28 http://www.met.police.uk/crimefigures/
    http://www.mcb.org.uk/library/statistics.php#1

29 Smith, as above, p28.

CONTRIBUTORS' BIOGRAPHIES

Avaes Mohammad is a poet, playwright, performer and analytical chemist. In 2005 he received the Amnesty International Media Award for his poem "Bhopal", broadcast as part of the BBC's commemoration of the 1984 Bhopal gas disaster. Avaes regularly delivers creative workshops, using theatre, rap, poetry and science, in education, community and organisational settings. Teacher-practitioner roles have included facilitation for the Unheard Voices writing programme (Royal Court) among others. As Associate Artist with London-based Tamasha Theatre Company, Avaes is currently leading the "Small Lives Global Ties" writers group, a group committed to exploring culturally specific writings as a means by which to attain universality. Avaes is an alchemist-artist creating challenging, provocative work in response to a challenging, provocative world.

Tim Sanders draws pocket cartoons and political cartoons, using the signature "Tim". He is a cartoonist for *Socialist Worker*, and in 1995 a collection of his cartoons was published as *In the Heat of the Scribble*. In 1999 Sanders began working as pocket cartoonist for the *Independent*, replacing Chris Priestley. As well as working for the *Independent* and *Independent on Sunday*, Sanders has drawn cartoons and illustrations for a range of publications, including the *Guardian*, *Observer*, *Daily Telegraph*, *Mail on Sunday You Magazine*, *Nursing Times*, *Broadcast* and *Red Pepper*. Sanders is also a Spanish speaker and a scholar of Hispanic art. www.timonline.info

Ken Livingstone is the quintessential London politician. The first directly elected Mayor of London from 2000-2008, leader of the Greater London Council from 1981-1986 and MP for Brent East from 1987-2001. At the core of his vision for London has always been that the city's openness, diversity and international population are a source of its economic strength and global pulling power. He has always seen multiculturalism and anti-racism as not just morally necessary but absolutely vital to the future well-being of the city and all its residents.

Hassan Mahamdallie is a senior strategy officer at Arts Council England and has a background in theatre and campaigning journalism. He writes on issues of race, religion and the history of black people in the West. Hassan contributed to the book *Tell It Like It Is: How Our Schools Fail Black Children* (2005). His biography of radical artist William Morris, *Crossing the River of Fire*, was published in 2008. He was a founding member of Unite Against Fascism.

Liz Fekete is executive director of the Institute of Race Relations and author of *A Suitable Enemy: Racism, Migration and Islamophobia in Europe* (Pluto Press).

Zita Holbourne is a member of the Public and Commercial Services (PCS) Union National Executive Committee, Vice Chair of the PCS National Equality Committee, a member of the TUC Race Relations Committee, co-founder and co-chair of Black Activists Rising Against Cuts (BARAC) UK, a national campaign group set up to campaign against the disproportionate impact of government cuts on black workers, services users and communities, and an award-winning performance and published poet and visual artist.

Tariq Modood is Professor of Sociology, Politics and Public Policy and the founding Director of the Centre for the Study of Ethnicity and Citizenship at the University of Bristol. His recent publications include *Still Not Easy Being British: Struggles for a Multicultural Citizenship* (2010) and as co-editor (with J Salt), *Global Migration, Ethnicity and Britishness* (2011). He is a regular contributor to the media and policy debates in Britain, was awarded an MBE for services to social sciences and ethnic relations in 2001 and elected a member of the Academy of Social Sciences in 2004. He served on the Commission on the Future of Multi-Ethnic Britain, the IPPR Commission on National Security and on the National Equality Panel, which reported to the UK Deputy Prime Minister in 2010.

Sabby Dhalu is Secretary and founding member of One Society Many Cultures, Joint Secretary and founding member of Unite Against Fascism. She has been an active campaigner against racism, fascism and Islamophobia for over a decade.

Danny Dorling is Professor of Human Geography at the University of Sheffield. He has lived all his life in England. To try to counter his myopic world view, in 2006 Danny started working with a group of researchers on a project to remap the world (www.worldmapper.org). His work concerns issues of housing, health, employment, education and poverty. He is an Academician of the Academy of the Learned Societies in the Social Sciences, Honorary President of the Society of Cartographers and a patron of Roadpeace, the national charity for road crash victims. Danny's recent publications include, *Injustice: Why Social Inequality Persists* (2010), *So you think you know about Britain?* (2011) and *Bankrupt Britain: An atlas of Social Change* (with Bethan Thomas, 2011).

Dr Edie Friedman was born in Chicago. A student in the 1960s, she was heavily influenced by the civil rights and peace movements. She came to England to study and subsequently worked for Oxfam and a community relations council in Leeds. She founded the Jewish Council for Racial Equality (JCORE) in 1976, of which she is now the director. In 2009 she co-authored *Reluctant Refuge: the Story of Asylum in Britain* and has written and co-authored race equality education books from primary to secondary levels. She is a regular speaker and writer on race and asylum issues.

Michael Rosen was born in 1946. His parents were both teachers and authors of, among other things, *The Language of Primary Schoolchildren*. They were political activists with their roots in the anti-fascist and Communist militancy of London's East End in the 1930s, which arose from Jewish socialist activity going back to the 19th century. Michael Rosen's childhood was spent in Harrow and Watford before university first at Middlesex Hospital and then Oxford in the period of the student uprisings of 1968, which saw him taking part in both the occupations of universities and the anti Vietnam War and anti-racist demonstrations. He worked at the BBC as a trainee before being sacked on the recommendation of the BBC's resident MI5 officer. From then till now, he has been a freelance writer, performer and broadcaster. He is now a professor at Birkbeck College, University of London. He has always been politically active, particularly in campaigns for fair and humane educational provision for all, anti-racism and anti-Zionism. Since 1978 he's lived in Hackney, London.

Gary McFarlane is a journalist based in London and has been a member of the Socialist Workers Party, and its forerunner the International Socialists, since 1975. He is also an active member of the National Union of Journalists, Unite Against Fascism and Black Activists Rising Against Cuts.

Benjamin Zephaniah left school aged 13 unable to read or write, but within two years his lyrical commentaries won him a strong following. His first collection, *Pen Rhythm* was published in 1980. Zephaniah has branched out into other literary forms, including plays and novels such as *Refugee Boy* (2001). He was the first to perform with The Wailers following Bob Marley's death, and at Nelson Mandela's request, Zephaniah hosted the President's Two Nations concert at the Royal Albert Hall in July 1996. In 2003 Zephaniah famously refused an OBE for his contribution to literature with the words, "OBE me? Up yours", at the time telling the *Guardian* that he feels "profoundly anti-empire".

Colin Wilson is a socialist activist living in London, where he is Secretary of Hackney Stop the War. He has written widely on LGBT issues, and is working on a book about Marxism and the history of sexuality.

Rehan Jamil lives in east London and is a freelance photographer producing documentary images relating to South Asian lives in Britain. As a recipient of a Leaders for London Millennium Award, he produced work for the book, *Common Ground: Portraits of Tower Hamlets* (1998), which documented the physical landscape and thriving community within the London borough of Tower Hamlets. Rehan is currently working on a long-term project relating to the Muslim community in Tower Hamlets and their lives around the East London Mosque. The mosque's expansion will qualify it as being the largest (capacity) purpose-built mosque in Europe. Rehan Jamil describes himself as a social documentary photographer who is primarily concerned with communities in transition.

Salma Yaqoob is the leader of the Respect party and an elected councillor for Sparkbrook ward in Birmingham. Salma appears regularly in the media and is the author of a number of articles on the British Muslim experience post 9/11 including, "Muslim women and the war on terror" (*Feminist Review*, April 2008), "British Islamic political radicalism" (in *Islamic Political Radicalism: A European Perspective*, Edinburgh University Press, 2007), and "Global and local echoes of the anti-war movement: a British Muslim perspective" (*International Socialism*, Autumn 2004).

Martin Smith is the national organiser of Love Music Hate Racism and a national officer for Unite Against Fascism. Martin has written extensively about racism and culture and his published works include *The EDL Unmasked, John Coltrane: Jazz, Racism and Resistance, Why British Jobs for British Workers Won't Solve the Crisis* and *Frank Sinatra: When Ol' Blue Eyes was a Red*. His new book on the BNP and EDL will be published in the autumn of 2011. He also writes a regular column for *Socialist Review* magazine.

Kelvin Williams says, "I spent my teenage years in a variety of institutions for relatively minor offences. As a result of this experience I have been a campaigning socialist and anti-fascist all my adult life. I moved to London 15 years ago and feel I have benefited from the rich diversity it has to offer, warts and all. I have a broad range of skills and interests but for the most part I am a lithographic printer turned photojournalist. I am a member of the National Union of Journalists and have spent the past two years photographing the EDL across the country. As such I have witnessed the racist and fascist nature of the organisation. I believe the EDL is fast developing into a no-boots-barred fascist street movement which must be stopped in its tracks".

Dilowar Khan is the Executive Director of the East London Mosque and the London Muslim Centre.

Yuri Prasad is a journalist for *Socialist Worker*.

Billy Hayes is General Secretary of the Communication Workers Union. The union represents around 220,000 members in the postal, telecommunications and financial services sectors. He was first elected to this position in 2001. He is a member of the TUC General Council, and TUC spokesperson on European affairs. He is Vice-Chair of the Labour Party's National Policy Forum. He is a founding member of Unite Against Fascism.

Weyman Bennett has been involved in anti-racist politics for over 25 years. He was one of the founders of Unite Against Fascism and is currently the joint secretary of the organisation. Weyman is currently working on a book about race and class in Britain today.

Mohammed Ali's work has been taken across the globe and described as challenging the oft-heard term "clash of civilisations", with his fusion of street art and Islamic script, along with his conscious messages. It was after his new-found passion and rediscovery of his faith in Islam that Mohammed, also known by the name Aerosolarabic, began to fuse his graffiti-art with the grace and eloquence of sacred and Islamic script and patterns. He describes his work as "taking the best of both worlds" and bringing back to the forefront principles that are gradually fading away from our modern societies. Mohammed has recently been awarded an ITV *South Bank Show* Award which recognises the best in British art and he continues to travel the world painting messages of hope, freedom, justice and love.

Contributors' biographies

USEFUL LiNKS

Unite Against Fascism http://uaf.org.uk/
Love Music Hate Racism http://lovemusichateracism.com/
One Society Many Cultures http://www.naar.org.uk/multiculturalism/index.html
Runnymede Trust http://www.runnymedetrust.org/
Institute for Race Relations http://www.irr.org.uk/
IRR Education resources http://www.irr.org.uk/education/index.html
Lets Kick Racism Out of Football http://www.kickitout.org/
Show Racism the Red Card http://www.srtrc.org/
Equality and Human Rights Commission http://www.equalityhumanrights.com/
Anthony Walker Foundation http://www.anthonywalkerfoundation.com/
Trades Union Congress http://www.tuc.org.uk/
Migration, Race and Population Dynamics http://www.ccsr.ac.uk/research/mrpd/
Black Activists Rising Against Cuts (BARAC) is on Facebook
The Muslim Council of Britain http://www.mcb.org.uk/
Muslim Directory: Islam at a Glance http://www.muslimdirectory.co.uk/iag.php
Muslim Heritage.com http://www.muslimheritage.com/

> *"The world is a dangerous place to live in: not because of the people who are evil, but because of the people who don't do anything about it."*
>
> **Albert Einstein**
> *Refugee from Nazi Germany*

Join **Unite Against Fascism**

Over the last decade we have seen the growth of racism and Islamophobia, and an increase in racist violence and attacks on multiculturalism.

This has culminated in the rise of far right and fascist organisations, in particular the Nazi British National Party (BNP) and the racist thugs of the English Defence League (EDL).

Unite Against Fascism (UAF) campaigns for a strong and united response to the far right from all those dedicated to freedom and democracy.

We aim to combine our forces and unite in a broad and common front against this common threat. We call for the broadest unity against the alarming rise in racism and fascism in Britain today.

Join Unite Against Fascism
Tel: 020 7801 2782 ● uaf.org.uk
● Email: info@ uaf.org.uk
● PO Box 36871 London WC1X 9XT

unite
against fascism

A Suitable Enemy

Racism, Migration and
Islamophobia in Europe

Liz Fekete.

Foreword by A. Sivanandan

'This book is a wake up call for all the
citizens with a sense of dignity
and justice.'
Professor Tariq Ramadan Senior Research Fellow,
Oxford St Antony's College

'Liz Fekete is one of the best analysts
of the complexities of racism today...
(This)is the major work we've been
waiting for. An enormously
accomplished and important book'
Professor Avery Gordon, Department of Sociology,
University of California, Santa Barbara

'This work of extraordinary
thoroughness and clear, passionate
moral insight provides a primer of
unparalleled utility.'
Gareth Peirce, civil rights lawyer

Available now from www.plutobooks.com
and in all good bookshops.

PlutoPress
www.plutobooks.com

IRR NEWS

An free weekly online alternative news service on race and refugee issues which seeks to give a voice to the voiceless through coverage of stories the mainstream media ignores.

A leading source of information on racism in the UK an Europe, with a well-organised set of resources covering a number of key issues, including:

- ■ Racial violence and anti-Muslim hate crimes
- ■ Deaths in custody
- ■ Anti-terrorism and counter-extremism
- ■ Asylum and immigration issues
- ■ Civil liberties
- ■ Islamophobia and the attack on multiculturalism

If you wish to receive regular news from the Institute of Race Relations by e-mail, please join our e-mail mailing list at: **www.irr.org.uk**

INSTITUTE OF
RACE
RELATIONS